STING SHIFT

The Street-Smart Cop's Handbook of Cons and Swindles

Lindsay E. Smith and Bruce A. Walstad

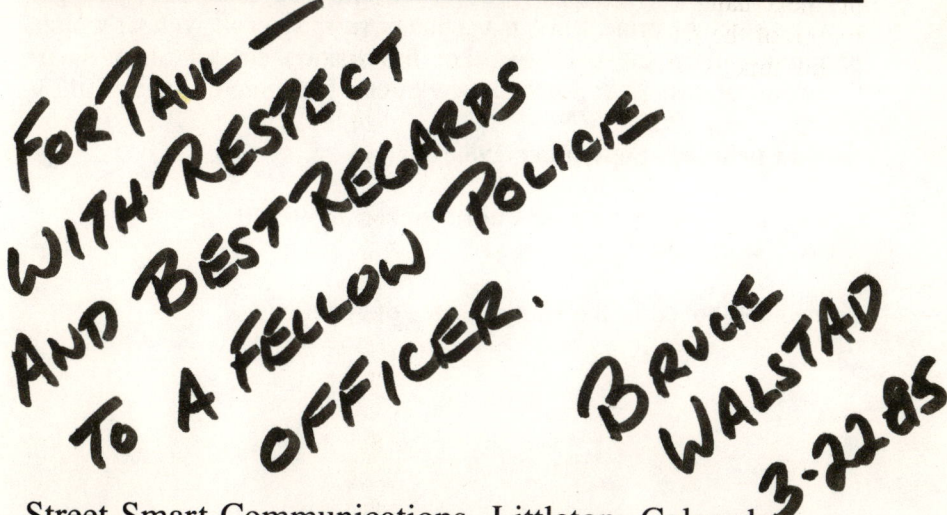

Street-Smart Communications, Littleton, Colorado

Important, please note:

This book is not intended to be a general indictment of any particular ethnic, religious or other group. It is intended to provide general background information on con games, swindles and other forms of cheating — some of which, as indicated, may involve individuals in certain groups or occupations. The incidents, activities and methods described in this book have been thoroughly researched by the authors to ensure their accuracy and completeness. The swindles described in this book are based on documented cases from newspaper articles, magazines, books, interviews, police files and first-hand investigative work.

The book does not deal with honest men and women. We're writing about crooks, con artists, swindlers, thieves and other assorted low-life individuals, collectively referred to by police as "the bad guys."

Neither the authors nor the publisher assumes any responsibility for the use or misuse of information contained in this book.

STING SHIFT. Copyright © 1989 by Lindsay E. Smith and Bruce A. Walstad.

All rights reserved. No part of this book may be reproduced or transmitted in any form or by any means, electronic or mechanical, including photocopying, recording or by any information storage or retrieval system — except by a reviewer who may quote brief passages in a review to be printed in a magazine or newspaper — without written permission from the publisher. For information contact Street-Smart Communications, 7275 South Depew Street, Littleton, Colorado 80123.

Second printing, September 1989

Library of Congress Catalog Card Number: 88-92840
ISBN 0-9621685-0-5

Printed and bound in the United States of America

Acknowledgements

The authors wish to thank the following individuals for their invaluable advice and assistance in the production of this book.

Al Cardenas, designer, The Creative Board, Denver; Ed Nies and John Wretlind, Mel Typesetting, Denver; Thomas Dobrowolski, banker, Chicago; Marianne Garehime, illustrator and artist, Denver; Ed Harris, artist and cartoonist, Minneapolis; Deputy Sheriff Glenn Hester, Sullivan County, N.Y.; Walt Hudson, magician and author, Baltimore; Lt. Larry Jones, Boise Police Department, and director, C.C.I.N., Boise, Id.; Chief John Millner, Elmhurst Police Department, Elmhurst, Ill.; and Detective Bill Polka, Park Ridge Police Department, Park Ridge, Ill.

Foreword

Discovering an area of rapidly growing concern in law enforcement, Lindsay Smith and Bruce Walstad have written an interesting, as well as practical, book that can be used as a guide to investigating con game-type crimes.

Making the best use of proactive investigative techniques, this book meets the challenges presented to law enforcement by the con-man criminals.

The topics discussed are grounded in a framework of experience and practical applicability. This collection of issues is encyclopedic and an indispensable tool for law enforcement practitioners.

As a police administrator, I am delighted to see this reference work written in a manner which can enhance the investigative abilities of an officer handling such incidents.

John J. Millner
Chief of Police
Elmhurst, Illinois Police Department

Contents

Acknowledgements	3
Foreword by Chief John Millner	4
Introduction	7
1 Cons and Swindles: Street of schemes	9
2 Prime targets: The elderly	31
3 The pickpocket: A "dip" in the crime rate	35
4 Shortchanging: Is this the perfect crime?	39
5 UFOs, "Big Foot" and other hoaxes	47
6 Fortune tellers, faith-healers and other fun folks	49
7 Gypsy cons and scams	69
8 Carny Knowledge	79
9 Twisting Satan's Tail: Cults and crimes in the world of darkness	97
10 Educating the Public: A one-hour community relations presentation	105
Resources	111
Glossary	115
Selected Reading	119
Afterthoughts	123
About the authors	125

> *"Son, no matter how far you travel, or how smart you get, always remember this: Someday, somewhere, a guy is going to come to you and show you a nice brand-new deck of cards on which the seal is never broken, and this guy is going to offer to bet you that the jack of spades will jump out of this deck and squirt cider in your ear. But, son, do not bet him, for as sure as you do you are going to get an ear full of cider."*
>
> —**Damon Runyon**
> ***The Idyll of Miss Sarah Brown***

Introduction

Runyon's advice, arguably the classic warning about proposition bets, is equally valid for many of the confidence games and swindles explained in this book. Generally, if a deal sounds too good to be true, it probably is. The opportunity that can't miss, can. Problem: not everyone believes that. That's why con artists are successfully working the streets today.

Con games. Hustles. Swindles. Flim-flams. Scams. Rip-offs. Different labels; similar results. Money changes hands. Advantage — the con artist.

Whether it's $1 lost to a shortchange artist working a football game or $5,000 lost to a team of pros working the pigeon drop scheme, it's a crime. And it's a crime that's going down on your street, in your town. Honest people are losing their money — frequently money they can ill-afford to lose.

We want you to know how carnival games can be rigged to give the operator an advantage. We want you to know how con games are structured so you can deal more knowledgeably with the victims. We want you to know how pickpockets work. We want you to understand the methods of the shortchange artist.

As you'll see in the following pages, today's confidence game field is a kaleidoscope of activities. Some, like the bank examiner scheme and the pigeon drop, are considered classic cons. Others are new, cleverly designed to take advantage of current economic conditions or some other contemporary event. For example, after the October 1987 stock market crash, investors in all 50 states were hit with telephone "boiler room" pitches to invest in (phony) gold mines.

In the criminal hierarchy, con artists consider themselves right near the top. As David W. Maurer points out in his book, *Language of the Underworld,* "Con men owe much of their prestige in the underworld to their use of intelligence instead of muscle." In addition, he adds, "There is an extensive technical knowledge on which the successful operation of a professional con game depends."

The authors are not conning themselves into thinking that this book, in the hands of law enforcement officials across the country, will make a serious dent in the cons and swindles that are going down everyday.

We hope, however, that this information is useful to the officers and investigators who are working, in large cities and small, to bring these criminals to justice.

And maybe, just maybe, it can help turn the advantage in favor of the good guys.

"Never give a sucker an even break."

—Edward Francis Albee
(made famous by W.C. Fields, 1930)

Cons and Swindles: Street of schemes

What exactly is a con game? How do con games work? Why do they work? Why do people withdraw hard-earned money from a bank account and turn it over to a stranger they met just hours earlier?

Think of a con game as a play — with actors and actresses, a plot, a well-rehearsed script and even a stage of sorts (on the street outside a bank lobby, for example, or at the victim's home).

Although the victim doesn't know it at the time, he or she is part of the cast.

The acting often is superb, the stage setting just right, the performance flawless. Curtain.

Basically, con games are a specialized form of cheating. Con artists usually have a method for controlling the outcome of the swindle.

Although some con games rely on the greed of the victim to be successful, others rely on the person's ignorance. Others rely on the person's good nature and desire to be of help. The old adage, "You can't cheat an honest man," doesn't always apply.

Con artists are clever people. They use many different methods to motivate their victims into believing in whatever scam they're unfolding. The victims usually are convinced that they are involved in a deal that cannot lose. At times, the con artist will use high-pressure tactics, like an aggressive sales person. On other occasions, the con artist will appear confused and uncertain about which course of action to take. It may be the victim who actually suggests what to do which, of course, is what the con artist was steering the victim toward all along.

In mannerism, speech and appearance, the con artist becomes

chameleon-like. They can be slow-witted bums on a street corner or upscale, articulate executives.

Often, depending on the scam, the con artist will show large amounts of money or valuables to the victim.

There are two broad categories of con games: the big con and the short con.

The big con is an elaborate and well-planned con that can be played out over a period of several days. It may involve several con artists all playing a particular role. It usually requires an extensive set-up. The best example of this type of con is in the movie, "The Sting."

A big con may involve a series of short cons all played out as one, leading to the final blow-off. Because of the extensive preparation, staging and work necessary, the big con is not one you'll run across every day. Also, the rewards for staging a big con have to be significant to make it worthwhile.

On the other hand, a short con generally takes anywhere from a matter of minutes to several hours to work. Usually there are just one or two con artists at work, although the number can go higher.

Victims are usually selected on the street or in a bank and will be taken for whatever they happen to have on them at the time, or for whatever cash they can get to within a short time.

All con games and con artists have their own methods and variations for the manner in which the con is worked. The explanations that follow are generic examples of how the most popular cons are worked.

Cons, hot and cold

Con games run hot and cold. A popular con can literally sweep the country, then drop out of favor for months or even years. Just because a con game isn't active now doesn't mean it won't be the hottest game in town six months from now.

If you were to plot the history of a particular con game on a graph, it would look like a roller-coaster: building to a peak of effectiveness, then dropping off into obscurity. But it never quite disappears. Someone is working it somewhere, changing it to fit the times and its popularity is on the rise again.

The Pigeon Drop

Contrary to what we just wrote in the preceding paragraph, this con never seems to go out of favor. It is worked by two or three people on the victim in this manner. One of the con artists, frequently a woman, will approach the victim and explain that she found a considerable sum of money and is unsure what to do with it. Another version has the victim and the con artist finding the money at the same moment. Quite often there will be a note in with the money hinting that the money was obtained illegally or is to be used for drugs. (When the participants later agree to divide the money, this message often helps them get past any guilt associated with taking someone else's money.)

The second partner comes upon the scene, pretending not to know the lady who found the money. She's soon involved in the conversation and is asked what should be done.

She explains that she works for or knows an attorney (or some other reputable individual) and says she will ask him what to do, and then leaves to do so. When she returns, she explains that the money can be legally divided among them, but one of them should hold it for a period of time (most often 30 days).

A conversation ensues, during which the victim is elected to hold the money. One of the con artists takes offense to that and explains whoever holds the money should put up "good faith" money for the others to hold while the victim holds the found money.

If the victim balks at that, one of the others will offer to hold the found money, thus allowing the victim to see the found money start slipping away. Once the victim agrees to put up the good faith money, the con artists establish how much they can get. Oddly enough, it turns out to be exactly the amount or percentage that the lawyer recommended.

Once the con artists finally have the money, they suddenly have places to go and things to do. The victim is left with the money, which always turns out to be cut-up newspaper, which was switched for the real money. Often, it is a stack of banded money which has a real bill on the top and bottom and the cut paper money or play money inside.

The Bank Examiner

This is another scam that always seems to be in vogue. The victim often receives a telephone call from someone who claims to be a security officer, a policeman, an FBI agent or some other bank official.

Sometimes the initial contact is made in person, just after the victim has left the bank. An "official" will stop the person, present some fake identification and ask for assistance.

In either case, the victim is led to believe that the teller who just assisted with his or her transaction is suspected of stealing from people's bank accounts, passing counterfeit money or otherwise manipulating accounts illegally. The "official" then asks for help from the victim in apprehending the suspected bank teller. (This is the scam in which the victim isn't trying to cash in on a sure thing; the victim is simply trying to be a good citizen and be of genuine assistance in helping to apprehend a suspect. Elderly women who respect authority figures are the most frequent victims.)

Once the victim agrees to help, he or she is asked to withdraw a certain amount of money from their account. They're usually advised not to tell anyone about the investigation until it has been concluded. In some cases, the victim is asked to wear gloves to avoid fingerprinting the bills.

Later, the official promises to send a police officer or someone else to the victim's home to pick up the money, or the con artist will pick it up himself. The victim is promised that after the money has been verified and checked, it will be returned to their account. Of course, once the con artist or his accomplice leave the victim with that promise, that's all he leaves them with.

Fortunately, more and more bank tellers are being alerted to the mechanics of this scam. Often, they're able to stop the scam on the spot by asking why the customer is withdrawing this large amount of cash.

Badge-Play Comeback

As if getting taken with the pigeon drop or the bank examiner scheme wasn't bad enough for the victim, there's a follow-up scam known as the Badge-Play Comeback.

After successfully pulling off a pigeon drop or bank examiner con game, the con artist will sell the names and addresses of the victims to other con artists who then work the Badge-Play Comeback. Here's what happens.

A week or two after the incident, the victim receives a telephone call from the new con artist (posing as a police officer). He acknowledges the fact that he's aware that the victim was the victim of a con game. He then informs the person that they have the con artists in custody and asks for the person's help. He'll either tell the victim that the con artists have the person's bank account number and the money is no longer secure, or that the teller at the bank is suspected of passing out counterfeit money. Either way, they need the person's help to finally end all this.

What happens, of course, is that the victim ends up withdrawing more money (supposedly to help the police) and that money, too, is gone forever. It's a cruel hit on someone who's already been victimized once.

Three-Card Monte

You may have seen a magician do this one, and it's a delightful thing to watch under those circumstances. The magician takes three cards, usually two black spot cards and a red Queen, and then puts a lengthwise crimp (bend) in them and with a tossing motion with both hands, he mixes the cards and throws them face-down on the table. You're invited to guess where the Queen lands.

You're always wrong — thanks to clever sleight-of-hand as the cards are tossed.

The con artist does the same routine — but invites bets rather than guesses on the outcome.

"A little game of hanky poo, the black for me, the red for you. All you really have to do is keep your eye on the lady. Ten gets you twenty, twenty gets you forty. Keep your eye on the lady." That's how the pitch started out by the old-time operators of this swindle.

Today, in major metropolitan cities, they work the streets on makeshift folding tables that allow a quick get-away when the cops are coming (they post lookouts).

Three-Card Monte hustlers also work major truck stops around the country, taking drivers for considerable sums of money.

Monte hustlers usually work as a "mob" of two or three people: the operator (also known as a "broad tosser" because of the action of tossing the Queen), someone posted as a lookout and a third member who acts as a shill to win money and get the crowd involved in the betting.

The big money in this scam comes at the end through a sucker bit. Unknown to the operator (?) the shill will put a small bend in one corner of the Queen — in full view of the assembled onlookers. Now the spectators are sure they can track the Queen and, accordingly, step up to heavy betting. It's a swindle. The operator, in tossing the cards, removes the bent corner from the Queen and puts the same bend in one of the black cards.

The move is amazing and absolutely undetectible in practiced hands — and believe us, these operators have practiced hands.

Three-Shell Game

This is similar to the Three-Card Monte. It's often seen on public transportation, done with plastic bottle caps. The operator moves three walnut shell halves around on the table top, hiding one small pea underneath one of the shells. Victims bet that they know which shell the pea is under.

In this one, sleight-of-hand again determines the outcome. The pea can be manipulated to appear under any particular shell. The game — as always — is under the total control of the operator. Victims simply do not stand a chance.

Hispanic Lotto Scam

The victim in this scam is almost always a non-English speaking Hispanic who is approached on the street for assistance. Some victims have said the con artist was from Colombia, others have said Puerto Rico. The con artist asking for help (also Spanish-speaking, of course) will ask the mark if he has heard of a particular lawyer. Usually he will give the mark a lawyer's name and some kind of address. A second con artist usually arrives on the scene at this time. He will claim to know the lawyer and says that he has a reputation for cheating Hispanics, especially those who are poor and/or uneducated.

The first con artist tips his secret. He has a winning state lottery number. He confides to the others that he is in the country illegally and is afraid to claim his winnings. He is convinced that the government will take his money and deport him.

The second con artist usually asks if he can cash the ticket for him. He almost goes along with the suggestion, then hesitates. He finally decides that the mark looks honest, and he'd prefer that he cash in the ticket. Con artist two complains that maybe the mark doesn't have any money of his own, and might just try to rip him off.

The con can go several ways at this point. Usually, the con artist will allow the mark to buy his ticket for whatever he can get. Or, the scam turns to a pigeon drop, with the victim's good faith money turning to shredded newspaper.

Block Hustle

Oddly enough, this short con is often reported to police even though the victim is led to believe he's buying stolen merchandise.

A con artist will bring his station wagon, van or pickup truck to the edge of a busy parking lot, shopping center mall lot or other area where there is an above-average traffic flow. Males tend to be the most frequent victims.

The back of the con artist's car or truck will be filled with new, sealed cartons of merchandise, frequently color TV sets, videocassette recorders (VCRs), compact disc players, radar detectors or whatever is currently popular.

The victim is led to believe that he or she is buying stolen merchandise ("All first-quality merchandise, never out of the box," they'll say,) but stolen merchandise just the same. Nonetheless, that's why the price is far below what you'd pay in the store, they explain.

One of the boxes will already have been opened with the item on display for the victim to examine. It's the real thing. A beautiful, brand-name VCR or whatever. And the price is amazingly low.

They agree on a price, the victim pays for the item, the con artist hands over the sealed carton and the deal is done. Only when the victim gets home and opens the carton does he discover that he's purchased a box of bricks and paper.

By the time he drives back to where he made the purchase, the con artist will be long gone — moved to another corner in another part of town to work the scam again. He won't stay long in one location, for he certainly won't want to be there when the mark gets back. And when the victim reports this to police, there's never any mention that he might have attempted to purchase something stolen.

Hot Truckloads

This con is similar to the Block Hustle, only it's worked on a store owner who is led to believe that he is buying a truckload of TVs, VCRs, microwave ovens or similar merchandise for an incredibly low price. Often, the owner is shown or given sample items.

In this case, the con artist usually accepts a deposit or down payment on the merchandise, and then never returns.

Jamaican Hustle

The Jamaican hustle is also known as the Handkerchief switch or the Jamaican switch. Typically, what happens is this:

The victim will be approached on a street by a man who claims to be lost, confused or in need of some kind of assistance. He will have a Jamaican accent, pretending to be recently arrived in the country.

The "foreigner," for example, may claim to have a considerable sum of money, but doesn't trust American banks because he's not sure he can withdraw his money once it has been deposited.

The victim is usually conned into demonstrating that, in America, funds are available for easy withdrawal at any time. He proves it by withdrawing money from his own savings account.

Sometimes from the beginning and sometimes later on as the scam proceeds, a second man gets involved. He appears to be a passerby, also intent on helping the foreigner. He brings forth a handkerchief and has both men place their money into it, demonstrating a safe and secure way to protect the money. Then he asks the victim to hold the money for both men and to meet back at this spot the following day at a specified time (since the banks are closed now).

Sooner or later, when the victim opens the handerchief, he discovers shredded newspaper instead of money.

In another variation, the victim will be conned into providing transportation to the foreigner, who often claims to be having difficulty locating a particular hotel. Usually a second person will arrive on the scene, and the Jamaican will repeat the story.

Eventually all three will be in the victim's car on the way to the hotel. En route, the Jamaican will propose a plan to double the victim's money. The victim will go to his bank, make a withdrawal and return to join the other two.

At this point, the Jamaican says he needs to run an errand. He convinces the victim to put his money into a bag which also contains the Jamaican's money. The victim is to hold onto the bag until he returns. The Jamaican, of course, never returns. When curiosity finally gets to the victim, he opens the bag to find shredded newspapers.

Latin Charity Switch

The Latin Charity Switch has many of the elements of the Jamaican hustle.

Here again, a foreigner with a heavy accent will engage a stranger in conversation. The stories vary widely, and a second person always joins the conversation shortly after it begins. Generally the dialogue ends up with a problem like this.

The foreigner is in town from (one of the Latin American countries) to settle the estate of his brother, who was killed in an accident.

It turns out that the foreigner has a large sum of money with him, insurance proceeds from his brother's policy. He is looking for a particular Latin American charity so that he can give them the money before he returns to his country. He adds that he would be punished if he returned to his country with this money.

He asks the victim if he knows where the charity is located. He has never heard of it, but the second individual explains that it burned down.

The foreigner says he has a real problem because he must leave the country, but offers $10,000 to each of the men if they will promise to find a suitable charity and donate the money for him after he has gone back to his country. He tells them there is $100,000 involved.

The second man offers to withdraw several thousand dollars from his personal account to prove that he can be trusted to do as the Latin American asks. The foreigner asks the victim to do the same.

Generally, the victim will go along because of the willingness of the other stranger to do so, and because he is demonstrating only that he's not doing this just for the money.

As in the Jamaican hustle, the funds are commingled and the victim is entrusted with them. Later, when he checks into the package he has been holding, he finds shredded newspaper.

Indian-Head-Penny Scam

This scam is generally worked in subways or train stations. It's also popular in hotel lobbies. New York City is an ideal location because of the heavy commuter traffic on trains in and out of the city.

The victim will be walking through the station or terminal, only to be accosted by a derelict who usually appears to be slightly drunk.

Instead of seeking a handout, however, the derelict presents a bank envelope containing various coins. He explains that he found the envelope and doesn't know what to do, and requests assistance.

The victim looks at the coins and spots an Indian-head penny that appears to be of value. There's a name and phone number on the envelope.

The victim suggests that the guy call the number, but the derelict refuses. Eventually, he convinces the victim to place the call.

Before he gets into an explanation of how he came into contact with someone who had these coins, a lady at the other end will become very excited. "You found my coins," she says. "I offered a $600 reward for them in the paper yesterday."

She wants the coins back, of course, but can't get a babysitter right then. Could the two men bring the coins to her?

The victim tells the derelict that the lady is offering $600 for the coins. Strangely, that's not what he wants. "I don't want to see anyone," he says. "I'll settle for $100 and you can have the rest."

The victim explains this to the lady on the phone. He only wants $100, he says.

The lady says, "Pay him what he wants ... and I'll pay you the $600 reward." The victim agrees to pay off the derelict and will collect from the lady tomorrow, since he's on his way home to his family now. All is settled.

The victim goes to a money machine and withdraws $100 from his account. The derelict explains that he's down on his luck because of booze and drugs. He adds that he wants to see that the right thing is done, but doesn't want to meet people or socialize. He takes the $100 and leaves, giving the coins to the victim who has plans to pick up $500 tomorrow.

The scam is over now. The phone number on the envelope belonged to a person who was the con artist's partner, at a pay phone nearby. The address she gives him over the phone is nonexistent.

Spanish Prisoner Game

The victim in this con is contacted (often by letter, but sometimes in person) by an individual who has a wealthy fellow countryman who is being wrongly held in a foreign jail. In years past, the person was always being held in a Spanish jail. Today, it could be one of the Central American countries, Viet Nam or Mexico.

He requires cash to bribe his guards or pay a specified ransom to leave the country. The rewards are varied, and always worthwhile. Treasure maps, valuable real estate property, a considerable amount of cash and other valuables are offered.

It becomes obvious as the scam unfolds that the prisoner has considerable financial resources — if only he can get to them — and they will be shared with the person who aids his escape.

The Obituary Hustle

This sets a new low in con games because it plays on a grieving widow or widower. The con artist reads through the obituary column in the daily newspaper and pinpoints the deceased by address, city and state. A day or two after the funeral, he will deliver, or arrange to have someone else deliver, a package containing some inexpensive item (frequently a Bible) purchased at a local store. The package is addressed to the deceased and arrives C.O.D. for an amount well above the actual value.

The grieving family, thinking that this was some item poor Charlie ordered just before he died, naturally pays for the package.

The Murphy Game

This one is rarely reported to police for obvious reasons. The victim strikes a deal with a street pimp (con artist) and then pays to have sex with a prostitute. The victim is instructed to go to a certain apartment or hotel room, knock on the door and give the password supplied by the pimp. The victim does as instructed only to find a vacant apartment or hotel room, or some poor person who has no idea what is going on. This con is most popular around hotel lounges or in areas where bars and taverns are concentrated.

Sealed Goods

This is another scam that is rarely reported to police because the victim was involved in what he thought was an illegal activity.

Through various means, the con artist makes contact with the victim, often near racetracks or illegal poker or dice games. The con artist explains that he has counterfeit money for sale and shows a sample which, in reality, is genuine U.S. currency.

If the victim indicates any interest, he is given a sample bill to keep and inspect. The con artist then quotes a price for a larger supply of the money.

When a deal is struck, usually at a later meeting, the con artist gives instructions to the victim about when and where to meet to make the exchange. The con artist may fail to show for the first meeting, explaining later that he thought he was being followed by the police or F.B.I. and did not want to get the victim in trouble.

When they finally meet, the con artist makes a big deal about being followed and acts very nervous which, in turn, makes the mark nervous.

The con artist has a number of sealed packages in his possession which (supposedly) contain the counterfeit money. Once the exchange is made — quickly, spurred on by nervousness — the con artist and victim go their separate ways.

Later, the victim finds the sealed packages contain only cut-up paper or newspaper.

In a variation of this, the con artist has one package of real money which he shows the victim. This is later switched for the cut-up paper.

The Autograph

This may be a con, or it may be just step one in another crime. The victim is asked for his/her autograph, for whatever reason. The victim may be a local celebrity of sorts (or just think he is).

Once the con artist has the signature, he can use it to commit a forgery, write checks or use it for other reasons.

The Drunken Mitt

This scam takes advantage of the victim's greed. The con artist enters a bar, and appears to be highly intoxicated. He shoots off his mouth about how he was a big winner earlier in the evening in a poker game.

He orders a drink and produces a big roll of bills and flashes it around, while bragging about how he can't lose at anything today.

He brings out a deck of cards and starts playing around with them. Then he'll challenge the victim to cut cards with him for quarters, or play some other penny-ante gambling game with the cards.

Once the victim is interested, the con artist challenges the victim to a game of draw poker. If the victim refuses, he simply deals the cards anyway. Once the cards are dealt, the victim realizes he has a pretty decent hand and, at the same time, he realizes that the con artist is trying to bet some heavy money.

The con artist "accidentally" tips his hand to the victim showing three Jacks, for example, which the victim knows he can beat with his hand of four Kings. Seeing some easy money coming his way, the victim takes the bet.

Strangely, the con artist discards three cards and draws three more to fill in a (now) winning hand with a straight flush. He shows the hand, picks up his winnings and walks out. This con is worked with a "cold deck" (one that has been switched into the game at some point) or the deck has been previously stacked by the con artist.

Put and Take

This is one of our favorites.

A con man goes into a bar during the late morning or mid-afternoon hours when the bar is quiet. He has a few drinks and strikes up a conversation with the bartender. He soon brings out a little "put and take" spinning top and challenges the bartender to play a few games with him for small change.

After they play awhile, with the con man winning most of the time, he tells the bartender that he has been cheating. He explains that the top is gaffed and shows him how to work it. By moving the stem of the top, it can be adjusted to land on either "put" or "take." Then he gives the bartender all his money back.

At this point the bartender is impressed, so the con man offers to sell the top to him for a couple of bucks, explaining that he has another one at home. After the sale, the con man leaves.

Several days later, a second con man comes in the bar — again at a quiet time — and strikes up a conversation with the same bartender. Now the bartender's greed comes into play. By this time, the bartender knows how to work the top and most likely has won some money with it.

He brings out the top and starts a game with the second man. The game goes on for awhile with the con man losing. The con man, however, keeps raising the stakes.

Finally, when there is some really big money in the pot, the con man switches the top for one that has a gaff that works in the opposite way of the one the bartender has. After the con man has won what he can, the game is over and the top is switched back.

Although the bartender may eventually make up his losses with the top on other customers, he'll be gunshy of that top for awhile.

The Priceless Pooch

Here's another scam that plays on a bartender's greed.

"Joe" enters a bar with a dog (no, not that kind of dog, a real dog). He explains to the bartender that he has an important business meeting to go to which will either make him or break him. He offers the bartender a few dollars if he'll just watch his dog for a couple of hours while he's in the meeting. He explains that the dog is a rare breed and should be watched closely because he's worth some money. The bartender agrees to watch him, and Joe leaves.

A short while later, Joe's confederate comes into the bar and notices the dog. He explains that he has a dog just like that at home and that this dog would be the perfect mate for his. He also confirms that this is a rare breed and offers to buy the dog from the bartender.

The bartender says the dog is not his to sell; that he's just watching it for another guy. The confederate emphasizes his interest in the dog and asks the bartender to see if the owner will sell when he returns for him. He names an amount he would pay, usually a considerable amount of money. Before leaving, he gives his name and address to the bartender.

A little later, Joe returns, totally dejected. He tells the bartender that he's wiped out, his business deal fell through and he's going to lose everything.

In an effort to brighten his day a little, the bartender turns the conversation to the dog. Depending on how greedy he is, he will offer to buy the dog himself or explain that another man came in who wanted the dog.

Naturally, the figure the bartender quotes Joe is nowhere near the figure offered by the confederate. Joe fusses and carries on about the low price and the fine dog, but eventually agrees on a price for this "priceless pooch." He takes the money from the bartender and leaves.

When the bartender attempts to find the confederate at the address he left, either there is no such address or the confederate is not to be found.

The dog usually has been found on the street or has been purchased from the city dog pound.

There are two other variations of this scam, the Violin Fraud and the Diamond Ring Scam.

The Violin Fraud

An unsuspecting store owner is the victim in this one.

A musician, quite obviously without much money, becomes a patron of the store, usually a small but prosperous store that handles general merchandise as well as musical instruments.

Over several days, the musician becomes acquainted with the man behind the counter. He makes a few small purchases, and runs up a small bill.

One day he comes in, carefully carrying a violin case under his arm. He explains that he'd like to buy a few small items, but has no money at present. He explains that money is due him in just a few days, and offers to leave his violin as security. Since his bill is so small, the store owner agrees.

The musician helps the store owner find an appropriate place to display the instrument, where it can be seen but not handled, explaining that it's quite valuable, although he doesn't know exactly what it's worth.

Several hours later, a well-dressed, upscale gentleman comes into the store. He has been there several times before, and exchanges greetings with the owner.

As he looks around, he suddenly discovers the violin. "A genuine old master," he exclaims, and asks the owner how much he will sell it for.

The owner says that the violin is not his to sell, but he'll inquire about it when the musician returns. The gentleman is disappointed and says he is leaving town for a few days. He tells the owner he wants that violin and will pay $500 for it, but adds that he knows it can't be sold without permission.

The owner tells the gentleman that he'll relay his interest when the musician returns and will set up a meeting.

The well-dressed gentleman explains that he's missed out on several good buys because he's found that musicians are a little strange sometimes when it comes to selling a cherished instrument. He tells the owner that if there's any way he can keep the violin there to do so. He encourages the owner to buy the violin from the musician, keep it there until the well-dressed man can return from his trip at which time he'll buy it from the owner.

He suggests that since the store owner knows the musician, he might be more willing to sell it. Further, if the owner can buy it at the right price, he will make a good profit on the deal.

Two days later, the musician returns. He's depressed. The money he expected didn't come through, he's overdue on his rent and has no other option but to sell the violin.

The owner explains that a man was in who wants to buy it and will be coming back for it. The musician says he can't wait, he needs the money now. He'll sell it on the street if necessary and be most appreciative of what he can get for it.

The owner sees an excellent profit in this situation. He offers to help the musician out by buying the violin. They negotiate on the deal, and finally settle on a price of $100 or so. The musician profusely extends his thanks to the owner for helping him out of his desperate situation.

After he leaves, the owner is pleased with the circumstances. He owns a valuable violin, and needs only to wait for the well-dressed gentleman to return so he can make a $400 profit.

The gentleman, of course, never returns. And when the owner finally decides to sell the violin elsewhere, he discovers it's worth maybe $10 or $15. Imitations of old violins are cheap, and the average person cannot tell them from originals.

The gentleman and the musician can work this scam within the same week with multiple stores in each town they visit.

The Diamond Ring

The victim is walking down the street, approaching a corner, when he spots the flash of some bright object on the ground. Just as he goes to reach for it, another hand reaches out and grabs it first.

The object turns out to be a ring, and the person who got to the prize first turns out to be someone down on his luck, living a day-to-day existence.

"Too bad, fella. Looks like a diamond to me. I'm gonna pawn it for 25 bucks before somebody comes around looking for it," he says.

The victim thinks that $25 is an incredibly low price. "You should hold out for a reward," he suggests. "It's got to be worth more than $25."

The finder says that $25 is plenty for him. He doesn't want to fool around with this thing, and says that he needs the money now.

The victim makes a quick assessment of potential profits, and offers $25 for the ring. The offer is accepted and the money and ring change hands. The ring, of course, is phony.

Not every victim will "bite" in the situation just described. Some people sense a scam in the making. So there's a follow-up twist to this one.

Just as the victim turns to walk away, the other guy says, "Hey, man, maybe you're right. It could be worth more than 25 bucks — but if I try to find out, somebody's gonna think I stole it. Do me a favor. Check with that pawn shop across the street and ask them what it's worth."

By now the victim's curiosity is aroused. So he checks it out with the clerk. "I can't really offer you anything now," says the clerk, "because the boss handles all the jewelry. But it's a nice stone and I've seen a lot of them. It ought to be worth maybe $300 or $400. The boss will probably give you two hundred bucks on it."

The hook has been set. The ring is real, and worth some big money.

The victim now returns to the guy who found the ring with one of two stories: (a) he tells him it's only worth $25 and the deal is completed, or (b) he levels with him and reports what the pawnbroker said.

In the latter case, the guy says he's afraid to pawn it because the cops will get suspicious. He offers to split the difference. "Give me a hundred bucks for it," he says. The two men barter and agree on a price, usually around $50-$75. The guy takes the cash, the victim gets the ring.

When the ring is later assessed by a reputable jeweler, it is found to be an imitation.

Here are the key elements in this one. The con artist plants the ring where it would catch the victim's eye. And he gets to the ring just ahead of the victim. If he can work the scam and sell it right away for $25, he's happy.

If the victim doesn't take the bait, the pawnshop ploy is added. For this to work, the clerk has to be in on the swindle because he will share the eventual profits. The clerk cannot be blamed later because he merely offered an opinion on the ring, and did not claim to be an expert on diamonds.

The disarming thing about this particular con game is the accidental setting.

The Pet Scam

This scam plays on the emotions of an individual or a family who has just lost a pet, usually a dog.

The con artist searches through the lost and found classified section of the local paper to find victims who have lost a dog. He'll call and report finding the dog and, because of the description in the paper, is extremely convincing.

The owners are delighted at the news, only to learn that if they don't leave a specified amount of money in a phone booth designated by the con artist, the dog will be turned over to a lab which conducts scientific experiments.

They leave the money, the con artist picks it up later, but of course the dog is still unaccounted for.

If this one becomes popular in your jurisdiction, other areas have had success in placing phony ads in the paper, then nabbing the con artist at the pick-up area.

Moving Day

Here's a scam that has been worked successfully in Denver as recently as August 1988 and in Florida, and no doubt in many other states as well.

In Denver, authorities arrested a 55-year-old man who was running one of the most popular scams in town — renting homes he didn't own.

The scam works like this. The con artist rents a house and then places an ad in the local paper, advertising the same house for rent.

As people respond and want to rent the house, the con artist accepts their payments for the first and last month's rent and, if possible, a damage deposit. The swindler provides them with (worthless, phony) receipts for their money and explains that the house will be cleaned, repainted and ready to be moved into within a week.

After collecting money from as many potential renters as possible, the con artist departs.

Only when multiple renters arrive the following weekend to move in do they discover the scam.

The Denver man was trying to lease homes owned by the Department of Housing and Urban Development (HUD) through a property manager. The manager contacted authorities when he learned that HUD owned the properties. Con artists will use any empty foreclosed home to dupe people out of a deposit and at least a month's rent.

The Missing Heir

Sometimes through an official letter, but more often through a phone call, the victim will receive notification that he or she is the sole heir of a small fortune left by Mr. "X" who recently passed away.

The con artist explains that a considerable amount of money is involved but, because the deceased died intestate (without a will), there are some complications with the IRS to resolve and some other problems to work out before the estate can be settled.

The victim is directed to send a "management fee" to the con artist who has been acting as an attorney or probate investigator. After receiving the money, the "investigator," of course, is never heard from again.

The Gold Brick Game

The Gold Brick Game is gone, at least the way it was played out years ago. But people are still buying gold in various forms (see Telephone Scams below).

Gold-brick swindlers were among history's most clever con artists. They would approach the victim, explaining to him that he could buy a gold brick worth $8,000 for half that price.

The story would be that the brick was stolen, or belonged to someone who didn't realize its true value, or was the property of a miner who needed the money, but was afraid to sell it openly because he'd be questioned about it.

The victim is taken to see the gold brick, often in a nearby town. He and the brick are taken to a chemist, who tests the brick and confirms that it is a real gold brick. The brick is placed in a suitcase and the deal is made.

As in many of today's con games, a switch was made. A duplicate suitcase, heavily weighted so it would have the same feel as a gold brick, would be part of the scam, and this suitcase would contain a brass brick.

The switch could be accomplished before the victim left the house or during the ride to or from the chemist.

The chemist, of course, is a confederate. If the switch already has been made, he tests the brass brick and verifies its authenticity. The game is played today with diamonds and zircons.

The days of the original Gold Brick Game are long gone, but this scam duped plenty of supposedly astute businessmen over the years.

Today, con artists are selling gold by telephone.

Telephone Scams

Telephone scams, run from "boiler rooms" (telephone sales offices equipped with banks of telephones), have been popular since the 1920s when they were used to sell worthless stock certificates.

Today, people across the country are being offered opportunities to buy valuable parcels of land; to lease property with valuable oil, gas or mineral rights; to buy silver, gold or other precious metals; or to invest in any number of other get-rich-quick schemes.

One of the newest swindles is selling "dirt pile" gold mines. It's been a favorite scam of boiler room con artists since October 1987 when the stock market crashed.

Here's the basic pitch. A high-pressure sales type will persuade someone to invest their money (usually $5,000) for 100 tons of "aggregate ore," guaranteeing that the dirt contains at least 20 ounces of gold.

The con artist goes on to explain that once the ore is processed, the proceeds will be passed along to the investor.

That appears to be a good deal, just on the face of it. You're buying 20 ounces of gold for just $250 an ounce, but it's worth approximately

$420 an ounce on the market (mid-November 1988). That sounds like a good way to nearly double your money.

The scam is that the dirt at the alleged mine sites does not contain any economically recoverable gold. Months after the investor finds this out, of course, the con artists have moved to another city to set this scam up again.

Authorities are calling this the "fool's gold rush of 1988" and estimate that Americans will lose $250 million in 1988 alone on this fraud.

Chain Letters

Chain-letter schemes date back to the Middle Ages when they were formed as "good-luck chains." Indeed, superstition continues to play a part in the schemes today.

Chain letters rise and fall in popularity, although there always seem to be several variations in circulation at any one time. They promise good luck to those who participate, and bad luck to those who break the chain.

Gambling authority John Scarne, in *Scarne's Complete Guide to Gambling*, suggests that perhaps women are more superstitious than men, reporting that the ratio of women to men participants in chain-letter schemes is 5 to 1.

The basics of chain letters are well known. A person will receive a letter, explaining how — if the chain is not broken — considerable wealth will soon arrive in their mailboxes.

"Do not break this chain," the letter says. "This letter has been around the world seven times."

A list of five names and addresses is at the bottom of the letter. The recipient is instructed to send $1 to the person at the top of the list. Then the recipient is to add his or her own name at the bottom of the list, remove the name at the top, make additional copies of the letter and mail them to five friends.

Since the U.S. Postal Service frowns on chain letters, some crooks attempt to circumvent those laws by circulating the letters by hand and mailing only the money. According to a bulletin issued by the U.S. Postal Service, that would also be a violation of regulations.

Con artists often start these chain-letter schemes, beginning as many different chains as they have time to write letters. Then, if they set up phony names and addresses as the five names at the bottom of the letter, they'll collect any money sent to them, too.

The Smack

The victim in this one is a tourist, checking out a popular local attraction. A stranger comes up, engages him in light conversation and they discover they're from the same state. In fact, they have a lot in common and the stranger offers to buy the man a drink.

They're engaged in conversation when a slightly tipsy gentleman comes up and insists on buying them a round. He's a bore, but the stranger tells his friend that he'll probably leave soon.

The drunk suggests matching coins to see who pays for succeeding rounds, and then suggests matching coins for a dollar or two to pass the time. The two matching players must pay the odd man. The stranger whispers to his new friend that if one of them calls "heads" and the other one calls "tails" regardless of what they toss, the drunk will always have to pay one of them. Although the drunk loses continually from here on out, he has no intention of quitting. Finally, in frustration, he says, "Winner take all. Let's play for one final round. The odd man will take the whole pot." The stranger tells his friend that they can't lose, and that they'll split the money later. They flip their coins and smack them on the back of their hands. (The con game's name comes from this action.) The drunk and the tourist victim match and both of them end up paying the stranger.

Eventually, the stranger says he has an appointment and has to go. The victim, anxious to have his money and winnings back, also decides to go. Once outside, the stranger starts to divide the money to give the victim his share. Just then, however, the drunk appears, sees what's happening and loudly exclaims that the two are a team of professional crooks who just cheated him. He threatens to call the police.

The two men try to calm the drunk down, and the victim is clearly concerned about the threat of calling the police. Both men insist that they've never met before today.

The drunk says that if that's the case, the two men should just go their separate ways — one down one way, the other in the opposite direction.

The stranger whispers to the victim to meet him back in the cocktail lounge in 30 minutes to divide the money. The drunk watches them go off in different directions.

The victim is back at the bar in 30 minutes, waiting for his friend. He'll have a long wait. The friend is miles away, busily dividing the victim's money with his partner, the "drunk."

Hot Seat Game

The Hot Seat Game is a short con in which the victim is led into a poker game where everyone present is in on the con — except the victim. Since there are so many people involved with this con, the cheating that goes on is practically undetectable by the victim.

What usually happens is that the betting continues at a fairly regular pace until, at some point, the victim is dealt one of those "unbeatable" hands. Now the stakes finally start escalating dramatically. In the end, as the players show their hands, the "unbeatable" hand is a loser.

The Tear-Up

This one usually is worked in connection with the Hot Seat Game. When the victim has all his cash in the pot and the raises are continuing, the other players agree to accept a check.

Then, when the mark loses the final hand, the con artist who won the pot will say something like, "I had no idea the stakes were going to get this high — and I don't think anyone had any intention of betting this kind of money. I'll be happy to settle for the cash that's in the pot. Let's tear up the check and forget about it."

He tears up the check, puts it in an ashtray and burns it. The victim, obviously relieved at what's happened, doesn't even seem to mind the cash he lost at this point. The surprise comes at the end of the month when his bank statement arrives. His torn-up check had been cashed.

The con artist carries any number of prefolded, blank checks in assorted colors. It's a simple matter for him to switch the victim's check for the blank check, which is burned. The tear-up is the blowoff to this scam and gives the mark a secure feeling that everything's OK. It also eliminates the risk that the victim might get to his bank and stop payment on the check if he thought he was being swindled.

The Last Turn

This is a classic big con wherein the con artist befriends a wealthy individual who has a love of big-time gambling. The con artist explains that he has a friend who works as a dealer at an illegal casino.

He goes on to explain that he and his friend have taken the casino for some big money simply by having the dealer deal him a winning hand at the appropriate time. He can't go back and win big again with the same dealer, he says, because that would be too suspicious.

They devise a plan for the victim to go to the casino on a certain day and time. He is to sit at that dealer's table and, on a designated hand, make a large bet which he will win. He then will split the money with the con artist.

The con artist brings the victim to the casino to see the dealer who even gives them a "secret" nod of recognition. All is set. Finally the big day comes and the victim, using his own money (which is part of the deal) goes to the casino.

When the designated hand comes up, a large bet is placed. Since it exceeds the house limit, the pit boss is called over. He approves the bet and the hand is played. The victim — how could this happen? — loses.

If he complains or creates a scene, the casino's bouncers physically remove him. When he attempts to find the con artist, he'll find that he is gone. If he later returns to the casino, he'll find that it is gone, too.

All the employees of the casino, as well as all the gamblers, have been part of this big con.

The Endless Chain

This scam also is known as On the Barrelhead because in earlier times, it was demonstrated on a barrelhead. There are several variations to the game.

Basically, the con artist takes a large loop of small-link chain and lays it out in a pattern on the table; sometimes two loops or circles, sometimes three.

The idea is for the victim to determine in which loop to put his finger so the chain will "catch." If he guesses wrong, the chain pulls free. During the demonstration, the victim is always able to do it. As soon as the money is bet, he can't. The secret is in the way the chain is laid out.

The Magic Wallet

A favorite of one of the old-time con artists was The Magic Wallet. He would pose as an important business executive, and presented it this way.

He had a confederate who would open the scam by finding a suitable victim and together they would "find" a wallet. Upon examining the contents, they would discover that it belonged to a VIP. The hustler, posing as the VIP, would come on the scene about that time, frantically looking for a lost wallet. He would be overjoyed when the confederate and the victim returned it to him.

Explaining that there were some extremely important papers in the wallet, the VIP/hustler would offer the two finders an opportunity to participate in a remarkable business deal of some kind, as a gesture of appreciation.

The confederate would immediately grasp the opportunity presented. If the victim was at all hesitant about joining in, the confederate would offer to buy out his share of the deal — putting further pressure on the mark to get in before he lost out.

Various business deals were offered and included such things as renting ball parks for the purpose of viewing Haley's Comet or selling bridges or businesses.

One of his strangest deals suggested that the victim could help out the president of the United States by purchasing secretly printed $100 bills for $50 each. The explanation for this was that it was done to run the White House, because the public would not tolerate the necessary White House spending.

The Country Send

At times, con games are combined to fit the needs of the con artist, the victim or the situation. The Country Send is a good example of that. Here's how it was used to swindle various farmers some years back.

The con artist befriends a farmer and gains his confidence. Shortly thereafter a second con artist approaches and offers to play Three-Card Monte with the two men. The first man whispers to the farmer that he knows the game and understands it well enough to beat this guy at his own game.

He and the farmer each agree to put up half the stakes for the game. The game takes place and, just as his new-found friend predicted, the two men win it all. The loser (con artist number two) agreed to pay off the bet ... but only after he saw the money that would have been paid to him if he had won.

The second man showed his money immediately, but the farmer had to go to the bank to get his out. When the farmer returned and showed his money, a switch was made. Then the loser (con artist two again) says he has to go to get his money to pay off the bet.

At that point, the original con artist says he will accompany the man to make sure that he doesn't run off without paying.

Of course, both men never return, leaving the farmer with a bank bag full of newspaper. You'll notice that two different cons (the Three Card Monte, and a version of the Jamaican Switch) were used in this game.

Comments by Walstad:

If you familiarize yourself with the manner in which each of these cons is worked, the next time you investigate a con game, you'll recall it from these pages. A quick rereading will refresh your memory.

Armed with this information, you may be able to assist your complainant fill in blank spots in his or her statement.

For various reasons, complainants forget or fail to include details of what happened when filing a report. One, they realize they have been conned and may feel embarrassed. Two, the complainant also may not recall the details because it was so confusing and happening so fast that he or she cannot reconstruct it. Or the complainant may know that he was involved in some illegal activity and is trying to report it while still hiding personal involvement.

(An example of this is the truck driver who has gotten involved with a Three-Card Monte game and lost a sum of the company's money. He can't go back to the company and report that he lost the money gambling, but he can say he was robbed or that a theft was committed.) With your understanding of basic con games and swindles, you now have an idea of what line of questioning to pursue. For example, the complainant says something like, "There was something to do with some found money in an envelope. Someone had to go call somebody else to see what to do, and then I had to put up some money if I wanted to get a share, and then everybody disappeared."

From this sketchy report, you'll know it was a pigeon drop. Now you can go back and fill in the missing pieces.

If you're able to make an arrest of a suspect, be careful in building your case. Intent may be hard to prove, and you may have trouble showing that a crime actually was committed. It's possible that a crime was not committed and that your complainant simply had been stupid and gave something away to someone else. Use good sense, judgment and knowledge in putting it all together. If in doubt, check with your local prosecutor.

In cases where you find that no criminal offense has occurred or if the crime is outside your jurisdiction, you may wish to refer your victim to another agency for assistance. See the Resources section, for more information.

Also, these agencies often can be of assistance to you in investigating your case.

If you have an opportunity to interview and/or interrogate the suspect in your case, you'll need a good measure of luck. For the most part, they're a tight-lipped bunch. One point to remember, as a point of attack, is their ego. The con artist usually has a big one; it may be your way to a confession. If your suspect refuses to talk about the incident, try talking about how other con games work. Explain that you're curious about how these things work. You might be surprised at how much you can learn. And you may loosen his tongue enough to get a confession. Remember his ego.

Here's a common ploy among con artists to be aware of. Frequently, they will get to your complainant in advance of the court date and offer a sum of money (well above the amount involved in the swindle) in return for dropping the charges. Warn your complainant about this possibility, because it will most likely happen. This may be illegal; check your state laws.

As with other types of crimes, collect all evidence and process it properly. If you're not sure what is pertinent, err on the side of collecting and preserving everything.

Many of the police officers I have spoken with regarding con games feel that the complainant deserves whatever he or she gets. There is some truth to this, but it depends on the circumstances.

If the complainant really knew what he or she was doing was illegal, then he or she does deserve whatever he or she gets, or loses. In other cases, as in the bank examiner scam, the person simply was trying to be of assistance to someone in need when the rug was pulled out.

Whatever the case, all con games and swindles deserve your full reporting and investigating efforts just as you would handle any other crime.

> *"Ever since Satan beguiled Adam and Eve with his apple trick, charlatans, knaves and confidence tricksters have flourished."*
>
> **—John Fisher**
> *Never Give a Sucker an Even Break*

Prime targets: the elderly

"Do you mean all that money's gone?" Tears welled up in her eyes. "But that was my life savings."

Too often, that's the unfortunate conclusion to many of the cons and swindles described in this book. Even more unfortunate is the fact that elderly members of society are the primary targets for cons, swindles and various types of consumer fraud.

According to Chicago Police Department statistics, the average victim is a female Caucasian, 72 years of age.

There are a number of reasons why seniors are the preferred targets for these scams.

- Seniors often have large savings accounts — from retirement funds, land or property settlements or insurance — and they make the tragic mistake of keeping large amounts of cash in their homes.
- Seniors are frequently unemployed which makes them more accessible to the con artist during the daylight hours.
- Elderly people are often lonely people. They're eager to talk to someone, to meet new people and to accept a friendship. Often, they're not as suspicious as the average person.
- Seniors are eager to help a person in need. Some cons are structured on that premise — the 'bank examiner' scheme, for example — and if that's the way it works, everything falls into place.
- Age (and unfortunately this happens to all of us) diminishes perception.

• Finally, seniors are sought out as victims because they are less likely to identify or prosecute the thief.

The problem is a serious one, but help may be on the way.

Illinois, for example, passed legislation in 1987 that would make "theft by deception," in which the offender obtained money or property valued at $5,000 or more from a victim 60 years of age or older, a Class 2 felony. (A Class 2 felony in Illinois provides for imprisonment of not less than three years nor more than seven years and a fine of $10,000 or the amount specified in the offense, whichever is greater.)

Most popular cons

Although almost any con game can be successfully worked against a senior citizen, some are more popular than others, for the reasons outlined above.

Two of the most common swindles worked on elderly individuals are the bank examiner and the pigeon drop, both explained in the preceding chapter.

Here's a third popular scam, generally worked by a young woman on an older woman. It goes like this.

The con artist will cruise a neighborhood during the day and pinpoint up to five or 10 senior citizens who may be likely victims for this telephone swindle. As she drives through the neighborhood, she'll write down the addresses.

Then she'll go home and use a cross-reference directory to associate the phone number with that address.

Next morning, at 2 a.m. or so, she'll call that number and wake the person with a routine along these lines.

"Hello, Aunt Mildred, is that you?" Aunt Mildred generally will respond affirmatively, to which the con artist will say, "This is your niece."

"Mary," she says, "is that you?"

"Yes it is. I'm sorry to wake you at this hour, but I've got a problem. I've been locked up in jail. The police caught me speeding and then found a gun in my purse. I'm sorry about carrying a gun, but with things the way they are today. . . well, you know how it is.

"What I need now is $400 bond (bail) money to get out of here. If you could just loan that to me, I'd really appreciate it. I have a friend — Louise — who can come over right now and pick up the money. I'll give her a call right now."

And that's the con. There is no friend; the con artist herself is the one who makes the pickup. Like other swindles, this one plays on the good intentions of the victim — in this case, a kindly aunt trying to help her niece out of a problem.

If the set-up fails for some reason, the con artist simply goes to the next name and number on her list and makes another call. The timing of the phone call is important, although the calls can take place at any time. Generally, when people are awakened in the middle of the night, they're not really clear about details or even who they might be talking with.

According to an article in the *Chicago Sun-Times,* Jan. 7, 1988, at least 30 elderly women lost nearly $10,000 to this scam since mid-October 1987. The figure is probably higher since many victims are too embarrassed to report the scheme to police. The article stated that victims ranged in age from 51 to 89 and lost between $100 and $500 each.

There are other ways cons can be played out on elderly people.

Consider the individual who is elderly and ill, perhaps terminally ill. That person will look everywhere for a health cure. After the family doctor explains the circumstances and the expectations, the individual is susceptible to a variety of other "treatments."

Perhaps a fortune teller will point the right direction. Faith-healers abound. Secret cancer cures are available. Even psychic surgeons might help.

Thousands of senior citizens are cheated out of their life savings every day by crooks offering miracle "cures."

Boredom is another problem. It's for this reason that we read articles in the newspapers about seniors signing up for lifetime dance lessons.

Item: A 69-year-old woman signed up for eight lifetime memberships consisting of 3,100 hours of lessons. The fee: $34,913.

Item: A 74-year-old woman sued a dance studio for the $25,000 she had paid for 2,480 hours of dance lessons. She was promised attractive male dancers and a chance to perform on television.

Item: A 71-year-old woman, who had a bad knee and could barely walk, mortgaged her home to make the final payment of her lifetime membership.

Investment frauds constitute another area where the elderly are targeted. Often they're promised that their investments are secure and that profits are assured. Yes, people are still buying prime swampland today.

Because many of these transactions are handled through the mails and by telephone contact, they fall outside the jurisdictions of normal police investigation. (Refer to the "Resources" section of this book to determine which agency should become involved if you encounter any of these long-distance swindles.)

The most common fraud being worked against senior citizens today involves phony and/or price-inflated home repairs.

Seniors take pride in maintaining their homes — neatly manicured lawns, well-tended flower beds, tempting vegetable gardens.

When home repairs go beyond the capabilities of the average homeowner, that's when trouble can occur. This is the perfect opportunity for the con artist to arrive on the scene, make the "repairs" (maybe) and then charge whatever the market will bear.

These are the most common home repair schemes:
- Driveway resurfacing,
- Furnace repair,
- Leaking foundations.

There's a spin-off problem here also. Some people will offer to do home repair and yard work simply to gain access to the home to steal money, jewelry or anything else of value.

Here's one example that has been worked in the Chicago area for quite some time.

Several guys will come to the victim's home and explain that they're surveyors. They'll have a long length of colored string with them, which they'll bring out.

They'll make up some story about why it's necessary to measure the property's footage and ask the victim to stand ("use as a measure," they'll tell him) at the lot line at the back of the house, while they run the string around to the front.

While one guy has the victim occupied holding the string, the other guy will be in the house picking up as many valuables as he can find. Eventually, they'll just tie the string to something out front, leaving the victim holding the other end — and they make their getaway.

The Elmhurst Press (Elmhurst, Ill.) alerted residents to paving scams being worked in the area in an article dated Aug. 31, 1988.

According to the paper, an 81-year-old resident was forced to write a check for $4,000 to three men who said they had done work for her (blacktopping her driveway). According to police, the driveway was covered with a black oily substance, not blacktop material.

Comments by Walstad:

Be observant. Watch for pick-up trucks or station wagons cruising residential neighborhoods where senior citizens reside. Be suspicious of similar vehicles, with a single occupant, parked in alleys or along residential streets. Watch for repair work being done on sidewalks, stairs or building foundations.

Get license numbers of suspicious vehicles, and run them through your department's system. You might be surprised at the interesting individuals (with long arrest records) you can turn up.

It's always helpful when local police departments maintain a good rapport with local senior citizen groups, and keep them informed about these activities through talks or meetings. (See Chapter 10 for a suggested outline that can be used by community relations officers.)

Check with the Better Business Bureau, the attorney general's office and the office of the local prosecutor to see what brochures and pamphlets are available. Many review some of the swindles mentioned here, and can be used as handouts during presentations.

> *"Among the most interesting classes of thieves is the pickpocket, whose clever subterfuges and skill of hand have been so often exploited in novel and story-book."*
>
> —**Harry Houdini**
> *The Right Way To Do Wrong*

The pickpocket — A "dip" in the crime rate

Pickpockets probably have been around since the day after the pocket was invented.

In the book, *Oliver Twist* — you did read Charles Dickens, didn't you? — pickpocketing was taught to youngsters. It's an age-old crime, and one that even today is taught on a person-to-person basis.

Here we're specifically discussing the pickpocket, also known as a "dip," and not the strong-armed robber who mugs people for their wallet and watch. There's a big difference.

Who is the professional pickpocket? What does he look like? Does he stand out in a crowd? There's no way to tell a professional pickpocket just by looking at him. They not only do not stand out in a crowd, they go to extremes to blend right in. The only way you'll know you've seen one is when you reach for your wallet and find it missing. Even then, you might not have seen him.

Primarily, you'll find pickpockets located in larger cities. You'll also find some of them travelling to follow large crowds or to work big events. In the case of major sporting events (like the Kentucky Derby or the Super Bowl, for example), some pickpockets will travel cross-country if necessary to be where the action is. Others prefer their own home towns and don't move around as much.

Some of the more popular places pickpockets like to work include: subway and bus stations, racetracks, concerts, sporting events and crowded sidewalks or hallways. Anytime a large number of people gather in a small area, you have the potential for pickpockets at work.

A lot of thefts will take place around baggage carousels at any major airport, particularly during peak travel periods.

On Dec. 22, 1987, Denver's *Rocky Mountain News* reported that seven wallets were stolen at Stapleton International Airport over the pre-Christmas weekend, most of them from people who were jostled in crowds and discovered later that their money was missing.

A racetrack is a particular favorite of pickpockets. At the track, they are able to stake out the payoff window and watch for winners. Here is the ideal victim: the pickpocket knows he has cash on him; better yet, he even knows where he put it.

Another favorite location is a bank lobby — for the same reasons. They can see the cash and see where it goes. Then they'll go for the money when the victim is outside the bank on a crowded sidewalk.

Pickpockets work on their own or in teams. A team may be two or more people who assist in locating a victim, jostling the victim and carrying off the wallet after it is passed to one of them by the person who actually picked the pocket. Another function of the "team" player is to bump or otherwise crowd the victim next to the actual pickpocket so he can go to work.

In his book, *The Right Way To Do Wrong,* published in 1906, the world-famous magician and escape artist Houdini writes, "It is simply amazing how quickly an expert pickpocket, with a delicate touch, seemingly accidental, will locate the resting-place of a well-filled purse or other article of value which he chooses to abstract."

Pickpockets practice their trade by using a store mannequin or tailor's dummy. The mannequin is dressed in the clothing the pickpocket wishes to practice with. The "dipping" is usually done with the index and middle finger or the thumb and index finger — depending on the situation and/or pickpocket.

"Just reach into that pocket ever so slowly, and..." — ding! Was that a bell? Yes. The old method of attaching small bells on the pockets is still used today as a practice method. When the pickpocket can get his hand in and out of the pocket without ringing the bell, he is in business. Your business.

Here are seven of the most popular pickpocketing methods:

Crime of opportunity

The woman's pocketbook is hanging halfway out of her purse. A man's wallet is sticking out from his back pocket. They're taken with virtually no effort, no skill. These are crimes of opportunity.

Whether these are actual pickpocketing incidents, as reported, or thefts by someone who could not resist the temptation is open to debate. It may have been the work of a professional, but most likely not. You and I could lift a wallet and get away with it under these circumstances.

The jostle

When you think about how a pickpocket operates, this is the classic method that comes to mind. Basically, the pickpocket bumps into the victim and dips him for his wallet. The victim does not notice the quick hand in and out of the pocket at the same moment someone bumps him.

This can be handled as a one-person operation or by a team. With a team at work, one person does the bumping while the other does the dipping. Often, a woman will bump a male victim while her male partner dips the pocket for the wallet. This is a nice distraction on top of the bump, especially if the woman is shapely and/or attractive.

Spills

This is an excellent method. The pickpocket will "accidentally" spill something on the victim's coat. It may be coffee, a soft drink, beer or whatever. Immediately, the pickpocket offers help and apologies. He may remove a handkerchief from his pocket and help the victim wipe off the spill.

He will certainly pull the coat away from the victim's body or help him take the coat off, giving him the opportunity to go through the coat pockets quickly and without detection.

He will remove anything of value. He may also dip into the pants pocket going for the wallet, if that's where it is. His cover for this is touching and wiping off the victim while helping him clean up the mess.

Cutting

This is an interesting method. The pickpocket uses a small razor to cut a slide in the pocket, allowing the wallet to fall out into the pickpocket's waiting hand.

This method needs to be worked in close quarters, on a subway or on a busy sidewalk, for example, where people are jammed together. One pickpocket who used this method was known to have a small piece of razor blade attached to a finger ring.

Bending

In this method, the pickpocket will be going for a man's back pants pocket. He'll either drop something on the ground or point out something on the floor to the victim. The pickpocket will have positioned himself so that he will be unable to pick up the object, and he'll ask the victim to get it.

As the victim does the bending (either on the up or down movement), the back pocket can easily be dipped for the wallet without the victim feeling a thing.

This also can be worked as a two-person operation, with one person doing the distracting and another doing the dipping.

Spitting

This is an old one, and somewhat gross, but quite effective. The pickpocket will spit on the victim's coat. Then he'll point it out to the victim, saying something like, "Geez, look what someone has done to your coat." Then this works like the spill.

If someone spit on your coat, wouldn't your first reaction be to take it off?

Wrist watch removal

To see this theft in action is unbelievable. Maybe you have. Some magicians include pickpocket demonstrations as part of their act, using a volunteer from the audience. This is generally one of the methods demonstrated because the reaction from the victim is so great. He simply can't believe that his watch has been taken from him.

In less than two seconds, just by grabbing the victim's wrist, the pickpocket has the watch. The victim never knows what happened.

The thief will somehow find a reason to lightly grab the victim's wrist, maybe while working one of the scams above or while asking the person to come over to see something.

The theft of a wrist watch takes one thing: practice. The thief must know and understand all types of watch bands. He practices by building an arm-like device that is positioned to the correct height. Then he'll practice by using different types of watches and watch bands, and practice removing them with one hand. Any why not? He's certainly got the "time."

Comments by Walstad:

As mentioned, pickpockets may or may not be working alone. Often, the second the wallet has been lifted, it will be passed to another member of the team who walks away with it. This is protection for the pickpocket, should the victim find his wallet gone at that moment.

Here are some hints when you're looking over a crowd. Look for people who appear to be watching the crowd. They may be detectives who have read this chapter, but more likely they are pickpockets who are searching for potential victims.

Watch for people who bump into others. Watch for drinks being spilled "accidentally." Watch for the pass of a wallet. Other than these tipoffs, it's hard to spot them — they blend in with the crowd.

> *"Ever since man invented money, he has been devising ways to acquire it easily. The means employed have been many and devious, ranging from the petty thief who steals pennies to the big time confidence man who steals thousands. One of the most clever is the short change artist."*
>
> —**Ralph Mayer**
> *Short-Changed*

Shortchanging: Is this the perfect crime?

It had been a long week for Frank, but finally it was Friday night and payday. He had been sitting at the local bar all evening, sipping beer and having shots.

At closing time, he picked up his change from the bar and walked out. He went home and slept it off.

Next morning, he counted his money and couldn't understand how he could be missing $20. He figures he might have spent $20 on drinks, but what happened to the other $20? He assumes it may have fallen out of his pocket and he lost it.

Frank doesn't realize he was the victim of a crime. During the course of the evening, the bartender shortchanged him out of $20. A dollar here, $2 there, and by closing time, the victim was out $20. The bartender knew the victim was intoxicated and wouldn't miss a buck or two.

Is this the perfect crime? Think about it. Here's an intoxicated individual who doesn't even know he was a victim. What more could a con artist want?

Suppose, however, that the individual notices that the bartender gave him the incorrect change. "Sorry, pal. Here's the other dollar." The perfect out. Shortchanging is almost the perfect crime.

Of all the crimes and scams described in this book, shortchanging is one of the most difficult on which to prove intent. The offender will always say, "Sorry, I made a mistake." Try to convince a judge or jury otherwise; it's just about impossible.

There are two basic types of shortchange artists. First, a person behind a bar or counter who shortchanges someone while making change (conning the customer) and, second, a customer who shortchanges a clerk by confusion or distraction (conning the clerk).

Conning the customer:

This can be just about anyone who makes change for you, from the clerk in the corner convenience store to the hot dog vendor at the ball park.

The most active shortchange artists are (in no particular order) bartenders, bar maids, street vendors, carnival ticket sellers and vendors and ball park beer vendors.

Did you notice that in three of the five categories, the sale of alcohol was involved? Why? An ideal victim.

Methods:

Here's a personal incident, experienced by co-author Walstad.

"When my son, John, was about three years old, I took him to a travelling carnival, which was set up in the parking lot at a local shopping center. He was having a great time, enjoying the rides and playing a few of the games.

"I walked over to the ticket booth where you purchase ride tickets and asked for three tickets (40 cents). I handed the clerk a $5 bill through the little opening. She pushed out the three tickets and 80 cents. I started to walk away when I realized I had another $3 coming.

"I turned and went back and my $3 was sitting on the counter just inside the booth. I didn't say a word; she just pushed the $3 out to me.

"My initial thought was, 'Lucky I remembered that.' Then, as I walked away, it struck me what had happened. She had tried to take me for the $3.

"Had I questioned her, she would have told me that I walked away too soon. After giving the incident some more thought, I decided to watch her for awhile. I stood off to the side where she couldn't see me.

"After about 10 minutes, a small boy approached and purchased some tickets. I didn't see how much money he gave her, or how many tickets he purchased, but suddenly he was loudly complaining that she had made a mistake with his change.

"She was telling him she had not made a mistake and that he was mistaken about what he had given her. He started to cry then, and really started yelling.

"Then I noticed a police officer approaching. All of a sudden, the boy was handed some money which he quickly counted. Then he walked away.

"I told the officer what happened with the boy and recounted my experience with the same ticket seller. He told me he'd take it up with the carnival manager, but whether he did or not, I don't know.

"I watched awhile longer, but then it was time to leave. I'm sure this woman (and others like her) do very well.

"In reconstructing this, I thought about the physical aspects. The ticket seller was in a small booth with a door on the back and a foggy, scratched plexiglass window on the front. A half circle was cut out of the bottom of the window. The change was on the inside.

"Standing in front of the window, you could barely see the person inside, much less the money on the counter. It was an ideal setup. My money was right there and I never saw it, until I remembered that I had more coming.

"This also works for another reason. Mom and dad are out with the kids for a good time, dad is trying to buy the tickets while the kids are yelling, 'Hurry, hurry, let's get on this ride next.' Mom isn't really too happy about this whole idea of visiting the carnival and has been 'discussing' it with dad.

"Dad is the perfect victim for this one. His mind is on everything else except getting the correct change.

"The other targeted victims are small kids or teenagers who are just too excited about getting to the next ride."

The incident described here is called the "Take it or leave it" scam, and it's a popular one for good reason. The "out" is perfect — "You walked away too soon, it isn't my fault." The individual working this one doesn't get rich on any one victim, but 50¢ here and $1 or $2 there add up to a lot by the end of the day.

The scam works just as described. Someone sells you something. You pay your money. Your change is given to you, but part is held back. If you stand there waiting for your money, it will be given to you. If you walk away too soon, you can be sure they won't call out after you to give you the rest of it.

The Billfold

This interesting method is worked by street vendors and ball park vendors. You've seen them — the vendor with a wad of money folded between his fingers, making change so fast you wonder how he can do it.

Here's the way this one works:

You're at the stadium, watching your favorite team, and you order a beer, hot dog, program or whatever. You hand the vendor a bill and notice that he keeps it separate from the folded bills between his fingers. He quickly counts the change right there, and hands it back to you. You put it back in your wallet or pocket.

You might just have been shortchanged. When the vendor was

counting your change, he had a $1 bill folded in half, end to end. He counted this bill twice. With a little sleight-of-hand move, this bill was unfolded and given to you with the others as the bills were being straightened out.

Most people, watching their change counted, won't bother to recount it, because they saw the correct amount going into their hand.

The vendor knows you'll never miss the $1. You want to complete the transaction and return your attention to the field.

He also knows if you question him about it, he can fall back on the standard "out" — "I made a mistake, fella. Sorry."

A crooked vendor, even just hitting every fourth or fifth customer, can do quite well.

The Holdout

In operation, this works much like the billfold scam, but it's done with coins. Here's how.

When the offender is giving coins in change to a victim, he'll count the change by dropping the coins from his left hand into his right hand, for example.

When the correct amount of change is in the right hand, the right hand is turned over and the coins are dropped into the victim's hand. The change generally goes right to the pocket.

So what happened? Sleight-of-hand again. Using a basic magician's technique known as "palming," one and possibly two coins are held back in the right hand as the change is poured into the victim's hand. Basically, the fleshy part of the thumb is used to contract and hold the coin(s).

Again, there's generally no apparent reason to recount the coins and, as you've seen over and over with shortchanging, "mistakes" do happen.

Five for Ten

This is a simple and bold method for shortchanging a person. When giving a victim change for a $10 or $20 bill, the offender simply gives change for a bill of a smaller denomination. $5 for $10, $10 for $20.

If the victim is preoccupied or intoxicated, he'll never notice the difference. If he does, it's the old story. "I'm sorry."

Miscount

Here's an equally bold method, best described by Ralph Mayer in his booklet, *Short-Changed,* which, by the way, was produced for entertainment and demonstration purposes and not for use as an instruction manual.

Mayer relates it this way:

"A man and his teenage son attended a wrestling show at the carnival. The man buys two tickets costing 50¢ each. He hands the ticket seller a $20 bill. The ticket seller gives him two tickets, then picks up a handful of $1 bills and counts them into his hand, saying, "Two, three, four, five, six, seven, say that's a fine-looking boy you've got with you. How old is he?" The man says, "Why he's fourteen." The ticket seller says, "By golly, he looks like he's closer to sixteen. Yes, sir! Sixteen, seventeen, eighteen, nineteen and the two tickets make twenty. Thank you."

"The victim crams the money into his pocket and goes in to see the show, completely unaware that the ticket seller not only stole the dollars between seven and sixteen, but also the last dollar."

There are, of course, many variations on these methods. These five seem to be the most popular.

Conning the clerk

Unlike the examples above (where the clerk or vendor cons the customer), here are several reverse applications. There are numerous methods and ploys used in this manner also. The objective is to distract or confuse the store clerk into giving the wrong change.

The Marked Bill

This is a two-person con game, worked this way. Customer #1 enters the store and locates a busy clerk. Customer #2 follows. Customer #1 purchases an item and pays for it with a $20, which has previously been marked in some manner — a signature, bank stamp, dirt or whatever. Change is given and customer #1 leaves the store.

Customer #2, who had been in line one or two back of #1, purchases an item and pays for it with a $10. Once the change is given and the $10 goes into the drawer, Customer #2 states that he's received the wrong change, and is $10 short.

The manager is called, either by the clerk or Customer #2. The customer explains that he gave the clerk a $20 and only received change for a $10. He says he can prove it because the bill had a mark on it, which he describes.

Once the cashier removes the bill from the cash register and finds the mark, the manager gives Customer #2 the other $10.

The manager is generally called to get involved because he or she does not want to create a scene. The manager will give up the $10 rather than take time (particularly in a busy store at a busy time) to question the situation.

Something Smells Funny Here

This is the same basic scam, except that Customer #1 passes a $20 that has been scented with perfume. Customer #2 is a woman wearing the same type of perfume. She explains that her $20 should smell of her perfume and, of course, it does.

$11 + Fast Talking = $20

The con artist makes a purchase of something that costs less than

$1. He pays for it with a $10, and the clerk returns the change, coins first.

As soon as the customer gets the coins, he turns to walk away. The clerk calls him back, and the customer pretends to be confused as he receives the remaining $9.

Then the customer apologizes for making such a small purchase with a $10. "Could I have the $10 back, in exchange for a $5 and five $1's," he asks?

He gets the $10 back first, then hands the clerk the $9, asking that it be counted. The clerk counts five, six, seven, eight and nine, and then asks for the extra dollar to make up the $10. The con artist pulls one out of his pocket.

At this point, the clerk has $9 and the con artist has $11. Here it comes. The con artist says, "Let's see, you have $9 there, right? Here's $11 more to make $20. Why don't you just give me a $20."

The con artist started with $11, ended (after a little fast talking) with $20, plus the change and whatever he bought.

Coins Across

A similar scam with coins is worked in this manner. The con artist walks into a store and asks for two quarters in exchange for a half dollar. He doesn't produce the half dollar until the clerk has put two quarters on the counter.

Then he puts his half dollar down, pushes all three coins toward the clerk saying, "Here's the half and two quarters. How about giving me a $1 bill instead?"

Reading through these descriptions you might think, "There's no way these methods could fool someone. They're too simple." Yet they do, everyday. And it's the apparent simplicity that's so misleading.

Comments by Walstad:

Shortchanging is one of the hardest crimes on which to prove intent. The offender will always use the "out," "I made a mistake, sorry; here is the correct change."

To show intent, you will have to establish a pattern. If you become aware of a certain individual you think may be shortchanging people, consider establishing a stake-out of sorts. Watch the person as best you can and observe the methods.

If you're convinced they're shortchanging people, you should plan to become a victim yourself. Why? How many times will a complainant show up in court because he or she was shortchanged by $1 or $2?

After you've been shortchanged, leave and document the incident according to your department's policies and procedures.

Then return, but not too soon to arouse suspicion, and let it happen again. Depending on the circumstances, you may want to take another officer to experience it. Use your own judgment. I would get at least three instances before making an arrest, maybe more. Check with your local prosecutor on this before starting.

Once the arrest is made, be sure to include the prior incidents in your report. You may be able to charge the offender with those also; again, check with your prosecutor.

Compared to other types of crimes, shortchanging may seem minor in nature. Viewed that way, it is. Yet it is a crime, a widespread one at that, and it does merit proper investigation, arrest and prosecution.

"The American people want to be humbugged."

—**P.T. Barnum**
American showman

UFOs, "Big Foot" and other hoaxes

"...but I'm telling ya, officer, this flying saucer just landed in a field down the road!"

When a call like this comes in, do you grab your partner, race for your squad car and hit the siren? Probably not. This is a hoax.

As if police officers didn't have enough work to do on legitimate cases, calls like these come in which turn out to be nothing more than hoaxes.

Dr. Curtis D. MacDougall, professor of journalism at Northwestern University and author of the book, *Hoaxes,* defines a hoax as "a deliberately concocted untruth made to masquerade as fact."

Hoaxes come in all sizes, shapes and colors. Some are too outrageous to be taken seriously. Others contain that seed of doubt so that people say, "Well, maybe..." Imagination has a lot to do with hoaxes.

Remember the toilet paper hoax? Several years ago, during the monologue on his late-night TV show, Johnny Carson reported that there was a shortage of toilet paper in this country. The next day, millions of people went to the supermarkets to stock up on toilet paper, causing a real shortage.

People commit hoaxes for a variety of reasons: financial gain, publicity stunts or political/personal attacks to get back at someone. Often, what begins as a simple practical joke gets out of hand. When that happens, the originator is sometimes too embarrassed to step forward and admit what happened — particularly when the incident is picked up and reported by the newspapers or when the police are called in to investigate.

If you're a police officer and get a call about some strange incident, you've got some questions to ask and some decisions to make.

Is this incident for real? Is this person telling the truth? Is this case unfounded? Does insurance play any part in this report? Is there a hidden motive here that I'm missing?

When you get a suspicious report, you might spot a hoax right away. Then again, you might miss it completely.

Police work involves dealing with many unusual situations and equally unusual people. Officers in just about every jurisdiction have learned to accept certain calls for what they are. Example: the person who reports he is being shot by invisible rays through a crack in the wall by men from Mars, or the elderly woman who reports prowlers late at night several times a week.

People report these incidents for various reasons. They may need to bring attention to themselves, creating a sense of importance. They may be lonely, and need the security of knowing someone in authority is just a phone call away. Others may be mentally disturbed, and may be having trouble dealing with the realities of the world.

Are you wasting your time when you are called on to investigate these incidents? Yes and no. Yes, because you could be out on patrol or handling other calls. No, because you're providing that person a police service, peace of mind or a feeling of security.

For whatever reason you get called into the investigation, ask yourself some questions in addition to those listed earlier.

—What, if anything, can the complainant gain?

—Is the press involved? (You should be immediately suspicious if you arrive in response to a call and find the press already there, conducting interviews and taking photos.)

—Does the complainant have a pattern of reporting odd incidents?

—Who are the witnesses to the incident? A brother, wife, friend of the complainant?

—Is there any real evidence? Is it missing? Was it destroyed?

Comments by Walstad:

The best advice I can give you is to use your own good judgment. My experience suggests that most police officers have a good deal of old-fashioned common sense. Use it.

Don't blow off any case or investigation just because you feel it might be a hoax. Follow your department's policies and procedures for disposing of cases.

If your investigation does reveal a hoax, you may consider filing charges of your own for filing a false police report.

Keep this information in the back on your mind next time you get an unusual report. With your suspicions sharpened, you probably won't fall victim to someone's practical joke or publicity stunt.

> *"Anyone who claims he can predict the future, tell you what someone else thinks or name a card in a shuffled deck is either lying, fooling you or working with a stacked deck. Anyone who tells you he has spoken with God or can communicate with someone who has died is crazy, a dreamer or a con artist."*
>
> **—Andy Rooney**
> *columnist and* **60 Minutes** *regular*

Fortune tellers, faith-healers and other fun folks

"I see in the crystal ball..."

Item: *Life*, May 1986. An article titled, "A Little Advice from the Gazers," accompanied by three color photos, notes that Angie Dickinson, Marlene Dietrich, Gloria Swanson, Spencer Tracy and Cary Grant all visited psychics for advice.

Item: The Sunday Magazine supplement of Denver's *Rocky Mountain News,* Jan. 3, 1988, featured a four-page round-up of local area psychics who offered their predictions for 1988.

Item: *Lerner Times,* a Chicago area newspaper, May 21, 1986, has an article headlined: "Psychic Fair to open at Harlem-Irving Plaza." The text reads, in part, "...her (Dolores Luciano, psychic) clients include stars of TV soap operas, athletes and politicians."

Item: Three Denver psychics, all members of the Colorado Psychic Center, were on Gary Tessler's radio talk show (KOA) just prior to Super Bowl XXII. Two picked the Denver Broncos to win, by seven and 10 points, respectively. One picked the Washington Redskins to win by nine.

All three used words like "tight" and "close" to describe the game, according to an item in the Rocky Mountain Skeptics' official newsletter. The Redskins dominated the game and embarrassed the Broncos and the psychics. Final score: Redskins, 42, Broncos, 10.

Fact: If you want help with love, money, sex, health, picking lottery numbers, having curses removed, improving your business or getting revenge, you won't have to look far.

Fortune tellers and psychics abound.

James Randi, author, psychic investigator, magician and lecturer, does not mince words when discussing the psychic field. In his book *Flim-Flam,* published in 1982, Randi writes, "Parapsychology is the respectable front of the fortune-tellers, gypsies, quacks, pseudoscientists and charlatans who labor to produce miracles and hide behind this foggiest of all philosophies."

How do you want your fortune revealed? Someone reading tea leaves, interpreting Tarot cards, reading your palm, gazing into a crystal ball or reading the bumps on your head?

Fortune tellers claim to see the future or tell you where you've been. You may be in law enforcement in this life, but you might have been a samurai warrior in Japan in an earlier life.

As we write this, the current "in" thing is "trance channeling," or "spirit channeling" or just "channeling."

"Channels" are personal spiritual guides who put themselves into a trance to communicate with someone from the past. These spirit voices then speak through the channel.

By whatever name, interest in the paranormal has always been popular. Yesterday: mediums giving seances; today: trance channeling. The authors, among many other skeptics, don't see much difference.

Although thousands of people claim powers of extra-sensory perception (ESP) or other psychic ability, their claims simply do not hold up under scientific investigation and scrutiny.

Interesting, isn't it? Psychics appear on late-night television shows demonstrating mind-boggling powers and abilities to a nationwide audience of millions.

Yet, challenged to perform the same stunts under controlled, scientific conditions in a laboratory, they quietly fold their tents and steal away.

Since 1964, Randi has had a standing offer of $10,000 for anyone who can demonstrate paranormal ability under controlled conditions.

In *Flim-Flam,* he reported that 650 persons had applied as claimants, but that only 54 had made it past the preliminaries. After nearly a quarter of a century, Randi still has his $10,000. He considers it quite safe.

His $10,000 offer, (the details of which are spelled out in Appendix I of his latest book, *The Faith Healers,* published in 1987), still stands.

The Fox Sisters

Some say that the beginnings of spiritualism can be traced back to two young girls, Katherine Fox, age 11, and her sister, Margaret, age 13, who lived in Arcadia, New York, in 1848. Indeed, they are known as the "founders of modern spiritualism."

The Fox sisters came up with a cute scam that made them rich and famous.

One of them would drop an apple tied to a string to cause a knocking or rapping sound on the floor. When members of the community came to their house, the girls discovered another way to produce noise. They would snap their toes against the end of their wooden bed.

They basked in the limelight as spiritualists for years. Even when the family moved, the spirits who lived in the house with them moved also.

The sisters eventually confessed their scam. Margaret exposed their methods before a fascinated crowd at the New York Academy of Music. Two weeks earlier, Kate had stated in print, "Spiritualism is a humbug from beginning to end. It is the greatest humbug of this century." It was all to no avail. Spiritualism was born and spiritualists were popping up all over the country. A fascinated, and gullible, public kept them in business.

Some working definitions

What's the difference between a psychic and a spiritualist or a medium? Here are some working definitions.

Spiritualist — A person who claims to communicate with the spirit of the dead. The spiritualist also is able to manifest the spirit's presence to the living.

Medium — A person who claims to bring forth the spirits of the dead and cause them, at times, to communicate with the living through the medium's body. The medium also conducts seances and causes the spirits to demonstrate their presence by lifting tables, having objects move or float around the room, have the spirits speak and sometimes actually materialize. (At seances, you can usually count on magic tricks being performed although they won't be described that way.)

Channeler — A new name for a spiritualist or medium, part of the New Age movement. Channelers usually will allow the spirit of a dead person or alien to come into their body to communicate with the living. Some channelers have only one spirit they deal with, others can have any spirit, including Jesus, available for questions.

Psychic — A person who claims paranormal power of some kind. It may be the ability to mentally move objects, predict future events, bend spoons (ala Uri Geller), transport themselves from one place to another on command, read people's minds, or locate missing or dead persons.

Astrologer — A person who predicts future events and provides advice on life, health, sex and/or money problems, based on the position of the stars and planets.

Numerologist — A person who predicts the future and provides advice, based on significant numbers in your life (age, birth date, number of children, etc.).

Cartomacist — A person who predicts the future and provides advice, based on dealing out playing cards in various formations and patterns.

Tarot card reader — A person who predicts the future and provides advice by dealing out Tarot cards in specific patterns.

Tea leaf reader — A person who predicts the future and provides advice by reading how tea leaves are positioned in the bottom of a cup.

Palm reader — A person who predicts the future and provides advice by reading the lines in a person's hand.

Crystal gazer — A person who predicts the future and provides advice based on what he or she "sees" in the crystal ball.

Fortune teller — An umbrella term generally used to describe any of the specialists noted above.

The "poor man's psychiatrist"

Why do people seek out psychics, fortune tellers and channelers? For some, it's a matter of curiosity. Mankind has always been fascinated with life after death and the unknown. For many, it's also harmless entertainment. (See the interview, "Confessions of a Tarot card reader," at the end of this chapter.)

For others, though, this is serious stuff. Some people won't make a decision without checking with their personal fortune teller or advisor for advice on health concerns, financial matters and their sex lives. These are people looking for answers in their lives. The old saying, "The fortune teller is the poor man's psychiatrist," applies here.

So what's the crime?

If a person voluntarily goes to see a fortune teller and pays for his or her advice, is that a crime?

Towns, cities and municipalities throughout the country have different local ordinances and statutes on the books regarding fortune tellers. In Franklin Park, Ill., for example, there is a local ordinance prohibiting any sign or advertising for mediums, psychics, fortune tellers and the like. Whether ordinances like these are infringing on someone's constitutional rights is an open question. At least in Franklin Park, it's on the books and has never been challenged.

Maintaining control

The point we want to make here is that you need to enforce the local laws. You need to maintain control. When a fortune teller comes to town and applies for a business license, you need to deal with that. Many fortune tellers apply for licenses as retailers or book store operators. If the application states one thing and you later discover the person is conducting seances instead, you may have grounds for rechecking the license and revoking it, if a violation is discovered.

You won't find many fortune tellers leasing a suite of offices in a downtown building, or occupying prime retail space in a shopping mall. Many will be running these operations from their homes which, in many areas, is illegal. Check your local ordinances.

There are other areas you can check to make sure that fortune tellers in your area are complying with "the letter of the law." Check for health, building and fire code violations in their building.

If fortune tellers are operating in your area and you want them to move on, research into your local ordinances is the way to get started.

So what's the harm?

Fortune telling is just harmless fun, isn't it? What's wrong with reading tea leaves for someone or gazing into a crystal ball?

Plenty. Once a fortune teller has the confidence of a client or victim, he or she is in control. Consider this scenario.

Mary Jones is a lonely person, currently going through a bad time in her life. She learns about a local fortune teller who may be able to help her with her problems.

Right away, "Florita" seems to know a lot about Mary and her problems, (using a method known as "cold reading," discussed later in this chapter).

After several costly visits, Florita is gaining Mary's confidence. Finally, she identifies Mary's problem: she has 'cursed' money. Florita asks Mary to bring in a modest sum of money and she will remove the curse.

Next visit, Mary brings in the money, Florita performs a strange ritual and the curse is gone. Mary's problems, however, are not. There must be some more cursed money at home. Next visit, same ritual.

Eventually, Florita comes up with the answer (and you don't need to be a fortune teller to see what's coming; you're way ahead of us on this one). "To solve your problem once and for all, Mary, bring in *all* your cursed money."

When Mary arrives, Florita acts "surprised" (delighted would be more accurate) at the amount of money she has. Florita tells Mary that, because there is so much to deal with, it will be necessary for her to stay up all night to remove the curse from the money. Mary will have to return tomorrow to pick up the money.

When Mary returns the next day, she finds the fortune teller has moved away, "forgetting" to return Mary's money.

Analyzing the crime

Let's break this down and see what happened. Florita was in business, looking for Mary or someone like her. While she was looking, she made a good living advising clients on a wide range of problems. Probably, she also sold various charms, trinkets, incense, candles and books.

In conversations with Mary, Florita learned a great deal about Mary's financial background through information she garnered in conversation and from observation (how Mary dressed and what jewelry she wore).

Florita worked hard to gain Mary's trust and confidence. (Does this sound like it has some of the elements of a con game?) Once Florita knew Mary had money and was exhibiting the necessary level of trust, it was time to go for the money.

After going through the cursed money routine several times, it was time for the big score. Mary was asked to bring in all her money, on the time and date requested by Florita, (so she could arrange travel plans and moving details). After Mary left on the final day, Florita vanished, only to pop up again in a new city or a new state to start the process again.

This particular scam is a favorite among the Gypsy fortune tellers. The scenario varies, but the end result is the same.

Victims in these scams are often those who can least afford to lose money. Here's a current example.

Denver's *Rocky Mountain News* reported (Nov. 7, 1988) that, in October, an unemployed laborer paid $4,200 to a man and woman fortune-telling team to cure his back pain.

On one of his first visits, the laborer explained his problems to the couple. One of them rubbed his body with an egg and when they cracked it open, there appeared to be blood inside, supposedly the bad spirit trapped in the egg.

Each time the man returned, the fee was higher. The fee was a fortune to the couple, but they borrowed everything they could because the fortune tellers promised that the money would return twofold.

When they went back Oct. 24 for another "healing session," the fortune-telling team was gone.

The paper reports that similar rip-offs have been reported in Miami, Kansas City, Peoria, Ill., and Los Angeles.

Fortune tellers abound in Los Angeles, where they call them "curanderas," or healers. Because of their transient lifestyles, they are difficult to find, according to Sgt. Jose Alcantara of the Los Angeles

Police Department.

Many use a mix of religion and voodoolike hocus-pocus on their victims, such as finding the "bad spirit" trapped in the egg.

Some other variations

Why some people refuse to share personal or financial information with friends or family members, yet feel compelled to tell a fortune teller they just met their most intimate secrets is one of life's many mysteries.

It can also be a basis for blackmail. Let's assume that a client, after making regular visits to a fortune teller, reveals the details of some past incident — an affair, or a criminal act, like embezzling money. On the next visit, the client hears those dreaded words, "Pay up or I'm going to the authorities with what you told me."

Blackmail situations can occur in other ways as well. For example, a male client attends a seance during which a nude female spirit appears. (You wouldn't expect a spirit transported from the afterlife to return dressed in the current fashion, would you?)

The next thing you know, the client and the spirit are involved in some sexual activity, which just happens to be photographed. On the next visit to the medium, the client is shown the photographs — strange how the image of the spirit can be captured on film, isn't it? — and is asked to pay up or else.

Here's another twist, this one playing on the investment theme. A client may ask the fortune teller about a business investment or a deal he's working on. Once the fortune teller realizes that the client is looking for a way to invest some money, he or she will "see" or "divine" a particular investment or opportunity.

(Forget the cash flow, debt service or other risk-analysis factors in analyzing a business; she saw this in her crystal ball — how could it miss!)

Not only can the fortune teller divine what investment to make, this seer can even provide the name of the person the client should contact. Now that's service!

As instructed, the client meets with the person and makes the investment: in land, a new business, a can't-miss invention or whatever. Of course, it isn't long before the fortune teller, investment counselor and the money are all gone. Fame and fortune are fleeting, aren't they?

Tactics to gain a client's confidence

Here are some of the most common tactics used by mediums and fortune tellers to gain a client's confidence.

1. Demonstrating powers, often through the use of magic tricks,

2. Creating problems, and then resolving them for the client,

3. Avoiding real problems by talking around them and not giving answers to them,

4. Creating mistrust of friends and family in the client's mind,

5. Instructing clients not to discuss their visits or the subjects of their conversations,

6. Learning all they can about clients through conversations, appearance and other means,

7. Working one on one — no audiences involved,

8. Frightening the client, to make them dependent on the fortune teller's ability to help them,

9. Using flattery,

10. Giving away small tokens or booklets on related topics,

11. Providing stories and anecdotes of past successes,

12. Performing unusual ceremonies to see if the client has been cursed,

13. Offering proof of religious training or background by presenting various credentials,

14. Using cold-reading techniques.

The last three tactics require further explanation.

Performing unusual ceremonies to see if the client has been cursed:

This happens in a number of ways. The most common include the following:
a. Rubbing "holy" water on the client,
b. Breaking open an egg and finding an unusual object (like a skull or a devil's head). "How would you like your skull, sunny-side up or scrambled?"
c. Placing a rag or cloth on the client's head,
d. Burning cursed money,
e. Burning candles to remove a curse,
f. Having a jar or glass of liquid change colors, indicating the client is cursed,
g. Chanting to remove curses,
h. Performing a seance.

Offering proof of religious education or training through various credentials:

We didn't want to "tip" this before now, but the co-authors of this book are both ordained ministers. That's right: the Reverend Bruce Walstad and the Reverend Lindsay Smith. The Rev. Walstad has more seniority by a couple of months (see "official" card reproduced below).

American Fellowship Church
225 Crossroads Blvd.
Carmel, California 93923

certifies that
REV. BRUCE WALSTAD

VALID UNTIL 9-6-88

has been ordained as a minister of the Church

Are you impressed? There's no need.

We're not talking about years of study, reading the Bible, religious training or even sitting in the back pew of a church here. We're talking $3 and a first-class stamp. If you can come up with that much cash, you can share this distinction.

We're mail-order ministers, and we did this just to demonstrate how easy it is to become an "ordained" minister. For $25 each, we could have ordered Doctor of Divinity degrees. Maybe if this book sells enough copies, we'll upgrade our status.

Meanwhile, we hope we've made the point that getting official religious documentation isn't all that difficult. In fact, Burling Hull noted in his book, *The Billion Dollar Bait,* that a reporter had his Collie dog legally ordained as a minister. That's why, when you're investigating a fraudulent psychic, and he informs you that you're dealing with a "man of the cloth," keep that $3 figure in the back of your mind.

Using cold-reading techniques

Because you've purchased this book and you're reading it now, the authors already know quite a bit about you. Here's our assessment. Ready?

"You are a friendly person. Although you have many acquaintances, you have few friends you consider really 'close.' People respect you. You are an emotional person. You are tense and anxious at times, and worry over little things. You strive to relax more. You tend to put off chores that do not interest you. You can be impulsive at times. You are thinking about doing some travelling. You consider yourself a clever person. You say things before thinking that you later regret. You are a generous person, but you also think you are materialistic. You don't like it when people look down at you."

How many of those statements apply to you? Our guess is that most of them do. That paragraph is an example of cold reading in its simplest form. It's a "one size fits all" profile. Too simple, you say?

If you could spend 15 minutes getting a "reading" from an expert trained in the use of cold-reading techniques, you'd be absolutely amazed at his powers and totally convinced of his abilities. But then, you're not that gullible, are you?

When cold readers give a reading, they first observe the client's general appearance. Is the client neatly dressed? Is the client wearing expensive jewelry, or an expensive watch? If so, maybe money's not the problem here.

Does the client seem unsure and hesitant? Maybe that's an avenue to pursue. "You're having difficulty determining which direction you should go with your life." If the client is overweight, a statement like "You are concerned about your weight and have tried dieting with little success," will generate a response.

Cold readers carefully observe how clients react to each statement. When cold readers "hit," they continue to pursue that line of questioning. When they "miss," they leave that subject for another.

Example: "I see that you've been having some problems with your wife lately." Slight nod of the head, so they go one further. "You've been arguing about something." Another nod. "She thinks you're spending too much money and too much time away from home." "Wow! Is this guy smart, or what?"

Cold readers will act as if the information is coming from another source or object, like a crystal ball, Tarot card spread or other source. Cold reading is one of the most important techniques a fortune teller can have as a demonstration tool. Cold reading is almost a "must" on a client's first visit. A skilled cold reader can expect that about 50 percent of their first-time visitors will return after a good cold reading. The art of cold reading has been passed down from generation to generation.

However, each of us uses some form of cold reading in our everyday activities. If you have some bad news to tell your spouse, you wait until you sense it's the right time to drop that into the conversation. "Oh by the way, honey..."

If you want to ask for a raise, you don't approach the boss when he or she's dealing with six other problems. You wait until a relaxed moment when maybe a compliment is coming your way. "I like the way you handled that last case, Barb..." "Thanks, Chief. That reminds me..."

If you've just met someone and want to get to know them better, pick out an attribute and make a comment. Noticing a fine tan, you say, "You must have just come back from a vacation on the beach."

You get the idea. Even in everyday conversation with your peers, you can tell if people really are interested in what you have to say. These are basic cold-reading principles that you've been using all along.

Comments by the Reverend Walstad:

On cold reading: At this writing, I've been a police officer for 13 years, four of them as a detective. I've done my fair share of interviewing and interrogating suspects and witnesses.

Several years ago, after learning more about cold reading, I tried applying some of the principles and techniques to interrogating. I was genuinely surprised at how quickly I was able to develop a rapport with people who otherwise wouldn't give me the time of day, and how much faster the confession would come when they started talking.

I started with just one or two statements, and now use many. Here's a general explanation of how I use cold reading in my work.

After getting acquainted with the person ("Hi, how are you doing? Do you want a cigarette or a cup of coffee? What do you do for a living? What did you think of that Bears game?"), I lean back in my chair a little and stare at them. Then I'll drop a cold-reading statement on them, maybe two.

If I get a reaction, I may pursue that and move on to one or two more statements. Then I stop the cold reading and start talking about why they're in for questioning.

My questioning/interrogating methods come largely from a class, "Interviews and Interrogations," taught by Chief John Millner of the Elmhurst, Ill., police department. In my opinion, Chief Millner has one of the best classes available on this subject.

As I continue with the interrogation, I occasionally drop in another cold-reading statement. No, this technique is not 100 percent effective. However, you can get to the rapport you need — and that needed confession — quicker.

One thing I found that works well is this. If a cold-reading statement strikes a nerve, but you can't seem to get any more from it, wait awhile and then repeat it, perhaps rephrasing the statement. You often will get what you need the second or third time around.

Here's another tactic I use. When the suspect is on the verge of confessing (head down, crying), repeat the most effective cold-reading statement that he reacted to.

You'll need to come up with your own statements to fit the particular situation, but here are several of my favorites:

You seem to be a troubled person,

I bet you regret things that you've done in your life,

You feel all alone, don't you?

I bet you are mad at your so-called friend for getting you into this,

You are an impulsive person at times and I bet that gets you into trouble from time to time,

You feel people don't understand you (great for teenagers),

You feel very frightened right now, don't you?

Cold reading works very well with sex crime suspects. I have a high success ratio interrogating sex crime suspects using cold-reading statements along with other basic interrogation methods.

For sex crimes, statements like these work well:

You know you did wrong, but you just can't help yourself,

You need help, don't you?

You didn't mean to hurt anyone; I know that.

Cold reading seems to work very well with juvenile, teenage and first-time offenders. Start practicing with suspects in these categories, then work up to adult suspects and repeat offenders.

One caution with this: don't overdo the use of cold reading. It can become too much for the offender, and he may suspect what you are attempting to do.

I have had great results using cold reading. One suspect, after he had confessed, mentioned to me that he was afraid to lie to me because he felt I knew everything about him. Don't overlook this technique. If you give cold reading a try, I think you'll be amazed at the results.

Psychic surgery

If, during your investigations of psychics, fortune tellers and spiritualists, you find a person who tells you about a doctor or psychic who performs surgery by placing his bare hands into the body of a patient and removes tumors or tissue without causing pain, leaving scars or wounds on the patient, you're hearing about a psychic surgeon.

Psychic surgery is nothing more than sleight of hand using magic props, animal tissue and blood and some good acting. Psychic surgery is regularly performed in the Philippines, but the "operation" is done in this country too.

The surgery goes like this: The patient may be prepared for surgery, depending on the psychic, by placing holy water or special oils on the body. Then the patient will have the afflicted area (usually the abdomen) opened by the psychic with his bare hands. The patient feels no pain as the surgeon reaches into the body and removes the tumor or diseased tissue. Blood is flowing from the area. After the tissue is removed, the opening is magically closed, the blood stops and there are no wounds or scars.

Miraculous, no? No. The psychic surgeon is a fake and so is this entire operation.

Here are the bare bones (no pun intended) of how this scam operates. The psychic kneads the skin around the area where he will operate, folding the skin to make a crevice. He then opens a small container of animal blood (often a chicken's) which he had concealed in his hands, allowing blood to flow around the area.

The psychic then pretends to push his hands into the body by bending his fingers away from the patient's view, in case he or she is watching. As the psychic reaches for a towel to clean up some of the blood, he is able to pick up some animal tissue or entrails which are hidden in the hand. As it is stretched out, it appears as if it is being extracted from the patient's body. After the tissue is put aside, the crevice in the skin is smoothed out, the blood is cleaned off and the operation is a success.

James Randi does a beautiful job explaining and demonstrating psychic surgery, and has done so on network TV.

If you find a psychic surgeon in your jurisdiction, you have a real problem to deal with. These people are doing absolutely nothing for the patient, except perhaps providing false hope. Terminally ill patients will grasp at any perceived "cure." Psychic surgeons will do nothing except put on their show and relieve the patient of (often) large sums of money.

The laws regarding this area probably are not those you are accustomed to dealing with. Contact your prosecutor for advice.

'Psychic detectives'

We continue to see newspaper and magazine clippings from around the country about police departments and other law enforcement agencies calling in so-called psychics to aid in their investigations.

Paul Kurtz, professor of philosophy at the State University of New York at Buffalo and chairman of The Committee for the Scientific Investigation of Claims of the Paranormal (CSICOP) says that a study by the Los Angeles Police Department showed that 'psychics' are of no value in solving crimes.

Kurtz says, "There is no hard data that self-proclaimed psychics have been able to help detectives in unearthing criminals or lost persons."

James Randi, quoted in a news release issued by CSICOP, had this to say on the subject:

"The 'psychic detectives' have created a mythology that they have the ability to solve crimes. In 1978, psychologist Martin Reiser conducted a lengthy study on behalf of the Behavioral Sciences Department of the Los Angeles Police Department. He carefully tested subjects who claimed these abilities and concluded that the police were wasting their time consulting such sources.

"Indeed," Randi says, "conversations with police officials involved in these procedures revealed that 'psychics' give them literally hundreds of 'facts' about each case, some of which are bound to 'fit' — but none of which lead to solutions.

"In many cases, since the 'psychics' are given details about the crimes and most prominent suspects in advance, they merely feed these back again in altered form, and then clamor for recognition of their abilities." Randi concludes, "...until police departments reject these charlatans as publicity-seeking clowns, the so-called 'psychic detectives' will continue to interfere with effective police work and to profit from the glory they borrow from such official association. Police have more important things to do."

The Committee for the Scientific Investigation of Claims of the Paranormal was formed in 1976 to investigate pseudoscientific claims. Fellows of the Committee include scientists, philosophers, writers, psychologists, magicians, engineers and representatives from many other fields.

This international organization also publishes *The Skeptical Inquirer,* a quarterly journal presenting a skeptical view of paranormal phenomena. (See Resource section for more information.)

Faith-Healers

A faith-healer is a person who claims to be an instrument of God or Jesus and that they have been given a special knowledge or ability. By praying for and sometimes touching an afflicted person, they claim the ability to cure the sick, crippled and dying.

Through the centuries, there have been many accounts of faith-healers performing miracles. Today you can witness these "miracles" in person or on television if you watch W.V. Grant, Peter Popoff, Richard Roberts and a host of other television faith-healers.

The advertising material and begging letters from faith healers include statements like "Expect Miracles," "The Blind See and the Crippled Walk" and one of our favorites, "Miracle of the Month."

Over the past several years, faith-healers W.V. Grant and Peter Popoff have been exposed as fakes and frauds on CNN, "The Tonight Show," "W. 57th Street" and in a six-part news special from WKOR-TV in New York. James Randi's 1987 book, *The Faith-Healers,* exposes the methods and operations of many of the more popular faith-healers in considerable detail.

There are many sad stories and tragic personal accounts of sick, crippled and dying individuals and their encounters with faith-healers. Scores of people leave a faith-healing service thinking they have been cured when actually nothing has changed in their physical well-being.

There are amusing stories too, such as the one reported by newsman Al White of WKOR-TV. He noted that one woman had her "invisible" short leg lengthened three inches. . . not once, but twice. Interestingly enough, she never noticed that one leg was shorter than the other, nor is one leg six inches longer than the other today.

Both Grant and Popoff have several special effects that they perform on their TV shows and in personal appearances. One is known as "calling out." This is where the faith-healer calls out a person's name, illness and sometimes their physician's name and then "cures" them.

According to Randi, Popoff was wearing a small radio receiver in his ear that he used to receive information from his wife's backstage location. She was reading the information from crib sheets gathered by Popoff's staff from persons in the audience prior to the service.

Grant is not known to wear a receiver, but is believed to have an excellent memory and uses it to advantage to recall the necessary information.

Faith-healers also gather information ahead of time through a common method used by magicians known as the "one-ahead principle." Faith-healers use this principle when gathering prayer envelopes from the audience. It's a mind-reading trick, but the audience believes it is seeing a real demonstration of power.

Another scam uses a wheelchair to demonstrate the "miracle cure." Elderly people entering the service, who are walking slowly or a bit unsteadily, are offered the convenience of a wheelchair by a member of the faith-healer's staff.

Then, at some time during the service, the faith-healer will approach the individual, "heal" them and have them get out of the wheelchair and walk — which they could do anyway. The audience, unaware of this, believes they have just witnessed a miracle.

Grant's leg-growing demonstration is a crowd-pleaser. Walstad witnessed this demonstration at one of Grant's Chicago services, and explains the technique. "Grant selects a person from the audience and brings them to the stage. He shows, through illusion, that one leg is shorter. Then, through illusion again, causes the short leg to "grow" even with the other," Walstad says. "This is done as follows. The person is seated on stage in a chair. Grant lifts both legs up and swings them away from the audience slightly, causing the back leg to appear longer. As he performs this 'miracle,' he simply moves the legs back to the normal position and the legs now appear even. The audience loves it," he says.

Although both Grant and Popoff claim success with their healing, they have failed to produce positive proof of their statements. Randi repeatedly attempted to verify faith-healing claims and was unable to do so.

The dangers in all of this are real enough. People who believe they are cured neglect advice and treatments from their physicians. Others throw out prescription medicines and fail to stay on their medications.

Faith-healing is a big business, although with the recent scandals involving televangelists, many have experienced financial difficulties.

Faith-healers are protected by First Amendment rights, and there is little you can do should a faith-healer show up in your town.

An aggressive investigative reporter from your local TV station may be interested in looking at the service from a more skeptical point of view.

Confessions of a Tarot card reader

Thomas Dobrowolski is low-key, well-dressed and conservative. He works in one of Chicago's largest banks.

He's definitely not the kind of guy you'd expect a woman would chase into a parking lot, begging him to tell the fortune of her pregnant daughter.

Yet that's exactly what happened following one session of reading Tarot cards at a neighborhood fair.

We interviewed Dobrowolski during a magicians' convention in Madison, Wisc., in October 1987.

Q. How did you first get involved in this, Tom?

A. I got a call from an agent asking if I could do Tarot card reading and fortune telling. I said I could, but at that time, I had no experience at all. So when I booked the show, I went to a local magic shop and bought a deck of Tarot cards and a book. This was about a week before the show. I studied for maybe a night, and made notes on how to read the cards on a piece of paper.

Q. Did you do anything special to change your appearance?

A. I thought I had to look a little mysterious, so I wore a dark brown shirt, dark brown pants, wore sun glasses and slicked back my hair — not greased back, but slicked back. The whole time I was there I gave the impression of being serious.

Before I went out there, I went through a process with the cards to make them look older, by bending them and by using shoe polish so they wouldn't look new — they looked like they'd been handed down through the generations. I didn't carry them in the case; I put them in a hanky. When I unfolded the hanky and brought the cards out, they looked like they were a hundred years old.

This also made it easier for me to mark some of the cards, since I didn't remember what some of the cards meant. The marks would blend in with the condition of the cards.

Q. How did you go about the readings?

A. The first couple I did, I had no idea what I was doing. I had notes written down right on the table to tell me different layouts and how the cards should be set out for a reading, but the people couldn't see the writing or tell what it was because of the angles.

I'd lay out a few cards, sit back in my chair with my fingers pressed together like I was meditating, then — because I had my sunglasses on — I could glimpse my notes to see what to do next.

Then I'd start the reading. After a few cards, I'd start interpreting what the cards meant, like good, bad or evil; health, love life or whatever.

Depending on the response, I could pick up what line to follow — it was basically cold reading. After the first three or four readings, I found that I could pick up things on people that were basically true, just from their reactions. They'd ask leading questions without even realizing it.

Q. For example.

A. I would turn over one of the cards and it would have the Cups and Coins on it. And I'd say something about money, which is pretty universal. They'd say, "I was wondering about that," so right away I know they have a money problem of some kind. And I know the problem isn't that they have too *much* money; it's not enough.

So right then I say, "I can see you're going through a difficult financial situation." You can say there's been a large financial expenditure that didn't work out, or that someone's just lost a job and — bingo! — you've zeroed in on something, based on their response. Then I'd follow that line through the rest of the reading.

Q. How long did all this take?
A. We were doing about five or six readings an hour, and I was there from noon to 7 p.m. with two half-hour breaks. I could have gone on reading all night; they were lining up.

I had one lady with a pregnant daughter follow me to the car to see what her future was going to be. I literally had to get in my car and drive away.

These are total strangers — people I'd never met before who didn't even know my name. I would start my reading, and they would pour their life stories out to me many times, asking for some kind of direction.

In the middle of one reading, a little lady came up — she had a real strange look — listened for awhile and then cried, "Oh, this is terrible, this is terrible. I've got the power ... I've been reading for 30 years, but this man has the gift; he has the gift."

Now I'm making all these readings up, but as soon as this woman said this, we could have used clubs to fight off all the people who began lining up for readings.

Q. How would you categorize the people who came to your table for readings?
A. Almost all of them were women, from teen-age girls through grandmothers. Most of them were middle-age and most of them were housewives — not real well educated, maybe high school but not much beyond that.

I would say these are people much more limited in life experiences — married young, had a family — where life focused around a family and their neighborhood.

One group I had a lot of was middle-age women with teen-age children, who were asking me things like, "Is this just a phase they're going through?" or, "Are they going to get out of this?"

Q. How about money?
A. The first time I did this I was paid a flat fee, and the people were charged $10 a reading. I didn't advertise there at all, because I didn't want people calling me at three in the morning asking me for advice.

At the first few readings, people would pull out $30 or a couple of $20 bills, ready to hand them over just like nothing for a 10-minute reading. They just assumed, or maybe read somewhere, that was the going rate.

After I'd finish some of these readings, people would want more readings, longer readings, private readings — and ask how they could get hold of me later.

I went into this viewing it as entertainment, but after I did it a few times, I figured I could go around to these neighborhood fairs, get a booth and make enough money in the summer so that I could take the rest of the year off.

Q. How would you respond when someone would ask you a specific question, like "Should I invest my money here?" or something like that?

A. I didn't want to give anyone any specific advice — I would have felt badly about that. My stock answer, my out, was to say, "I'm not telling you what to do; I can't tell you what to do. All I can tell you is what the cards are telling me." This eased my conscience.

But you have to realize that these people believe in you and believe in the cards. They're going to do whatever you say, whatever you tell them to do.

Q. Even something outrageous?

A. Yes. I honestly think that if I told people to do something truly outrageous, they would have done it. I had a couple of instances where people — after I'd finished the reading — said, "That's just right on. Now, I know what the cards say, but would you advise me then that it *would* be a good idea to move out on my husband?" And I'd say, "I can't tell you that. You have to decide for yourself."

These are complete strangers, telling me things they wouldn't tell anyone else. I'm just a guy in dark glasses, sitting at a table, and they're spilling everything they have to me.

Q. How long did you do this, and how did your views of Tarot card reading change during this period?

A. I did this on six or eight different occasions over a period of a year and a half.

I was so intrigued by it that I went out after the first week and got a couple more books on Tarot and started reading more for background. I could see how you could really get involved and start believing that you have a power. I got out because I felt dirty doing what I was doing.

You'd start hitting on things in a person's life — cold reading — and after you'd hit four or fives times, you start to think that maybe there is something to this.

You start to become proficient real quickly. It's really basic psychology, but you start to believe that maybe there's something more here. You get to the point where you have to bring yourself back down to reality and say, "No, no, no ... this is all hype."

Q. You also did private parties. How did those work?

A. Basically, these were adult cocktail or dinner parties, with five to 10 couples at someone's home. They'd call me for entertainment.

While they were having drinks or dinner, I'd set up my table, covered with a cloth and a pad on top, in a separate room like the family room or a library. Then they'd come in either individually or as a couple and I'd give them a reading.

I'd stay for an hour or two until everyone who wanted a reading had one. Then I'd charge the people who were having the party $30 a person for those who had a reading.

Q. Any final comments?

A. The reason I got out was that I felt dirty. I saw ways to make a lot of money, but I didn't feel good about it.

If you go in as a performer, like a magician, and you do a show, everyone knows it's entertainment. They have a good time and they pay you. The problem I had with Tarot card reading is that a lot of people don't view this as entertainment, and I felt I was taking money under false pretenses. Although the money was good, my conscience got to me after awhile.

I think half the people who read Tarot cards honestly believe they have some kind of power — but I think the other half are strictly con artists. They know this is a bunch of crap and they just want to get their money and move on.

This is more common than people realize; it's thriving. People are looking for answers to a lot of questions in their lives, and they're more into this kind of thing than ever before. And it crosses all people — rich, poor, young and old — throughout our society.

> *"If you ask twenty Gypsies the same question, you will get twenty different answers. On the other hand, if you ask one Gypsy the same question twenty times, you will still get twenty different answers."*
>
> —Old saying

Gypsy Cons and Scams

If that saying leads you to believe that you will never understand the Gypsy culture, you're probably right. On the other hand, if you think that saying leads you to believe you understand the Gypsy culture, you're probably right too.

Stay with us; you'll find this is an interesting chapter.

Note: All references to Gypsies throughout this chapter are intended to include only that segment of the Gypsy population that has chosen to engage in criminal activities. Not all Gypsies are criminals, nor are all Gypsies engaged in the frauds and scams discussed in this chapter. There are honest and law-abiding Gypsies who have assimilated into our culture. But yet that statement creates a paradox. Using Gypsy standards, any Gypsy who fully assimilates into our culture is no longer considered to be a true Gypsy.

For Gypsies who have chosen a life of crime, the basic question is, "Why do Gypsies steal?"

One answer lies in the legend that has been handed down through the generations. It goes like this:

Traditionally, Gypsies were blacksmiths. As such, they were commissioned by Roman soldiers to make four nails to be used for the crucifixion of Jesus Christ. After making the nails, the Gypsies went to bed and woke the next morning to find the fourth nail glowing.

An angel came and told the Gypsies that this nail was supposed to be used to kill Jesus, by driving it through His heart. According to the legend, a small Gypsy boy stole the nail. Jesus supposedly told the Gypsies that since this boy stole the nail to save Him from pain, the Gypsies could steal forever and ever.

Here's another version of this story:

Jesus was going to be crucified and a Gypsy blacksmith, a slave, was ordered by the Roman soldiers to make four nails, three to go into His hands and feet and one through His heart. The Gypsy stalled and stalled, but the soldier whipped him so he made the four nails. He asked God to help him and to help the Gypsies. God cried and the Gypsy cried. When he was to deliver the nails, he swallowed one and told the soldiers he had lost it.

When God saw that he had swallowed the nail intended for Jesus' heart, He said, "Gypsy, you are free to go and travel anywhere and you can steal your food and take what you need to live." And that is why Gypsies travel and why they steal.

The Gypsies don't have any proof of these legends, you understand, so you can treat Gypsy crimes the same as any other you encounter.

How many Gypsies are there? James Yuenger, in an article in *The Chicago Tribune,* (Sept. 20, 1987) titled, "Gypsies: The last outsiders" writes, "There are no reliable statistics. It is generally thought that there are three to five million Gypsies worldwide, about one million of them in North America and 5,000 to 10,000 of them in the Chicago area. Those figures have been circulating unchecked for years, however, and the Gypsies' refusal to be counted makes it impossible for authorities to update them."

There are two types of Gypsies: American Gypsies and European Gypsies. According to various studies, American Gypsies are mostly involved in home repair, black topping, tree trimming and similar types of business scams.

European Gypsies are primarily involved in home invasions, store diversions and shoplifting.

These classifications have no meaning to Gypsies, nor do national identities such as Polish, Yugoslavian, German or Russian, according to Terry Getsay, a criminal justice analyst with the Illinois Department of Law Enforcement and an expert on the Gypsy culture. Getsay has authored several articles on the criminal activities of Gypsies, and is frequently requested to conduct seminars on the subject for law enforcement agencies.

Gypsy culture and beliefs

Gypsies have no written language and, for the most part, are illiterate. Many still speak their native tongue, Romani.

As expected, Gypsies do keep on the move for the most part — around the country, from town to town or from apartment to apartment within a city. Traveling is considered to bring good luck and good health.

Gypsies who violate the rules of Gypsy culture are considered to be in a state of "marime," (meaning pollution or defilement). If caught in a "marime" violation, the Gypsy is no longer allowed to eat, sleep or communicate with other Gypsies. There are only a few ways out of the situation. One is through a trial with other Gypsies who serve as judge and jury, a second is simply through an elapse of time of "marime" and another is through a payoff to the elders for forgiveness.

In some family structures or clans, there may be a head man, or chief, who settles disputes, pays bail bonds and fines and handles legal matters.

Homosexuality and rape are not tolerated.

Gypsies believe that the head is a sacred part of the body and that nothing must pass over it. Males who have large heads are considered to have good luck and good looks.

Food, cooking and eating utensils are handled with extreme care to ensure cleanliness. Anything that falls on the floor is "marime." Each Gypsy has an individual set of dishes and silverware that is never used by anyone else.

As a general rule, they do not trust police officers, nor do they have respect for the criminal justice system. Many believe police officers can be bought off. Curiously though, when feuding with other Gypsies, they will furnish information to the police about the location and M.O. of Gypsies committing crimes.

They consider "gaje" (non-Gypsies) to be dirty sub-human creatures that are to be avoided as much as possible. They have great respect for their elders. Both men and women marry young; women often between the ages of 10 and 18, and men between the ages of 13 and 20. The Gypsy male is responsible for the actions of his wife and children. When a daughter leaves to be married, she becomes part of her husband's family.

Gypsies do not like steady employment, nor do they like working with non-Gypsies.

Home Repairs

These scams are generally worked as follows. A Gypsy or Gypsies will approach the mark (usually an elderly person) at his or her home. They will offer to make home repairs, such as driveway seal coating, electrical work, roofing work or whatever.

A fee is agreed upon and some sort of work will be done, although far from what the homeowner would consider quality work.

At this point, several things can happen. The Gypsies can take the money and leave, explain that the job was more involved or time-consuming than originally estimated and that the cost will be much higher, or tell the homeowner they have found other things around the house needing immediate attention which can be repaired for an additional fee.

Some of the more popular scams worked by Gypsies include:

—Driveway seal coating, using watered-down sealant or automotive drain oil, (the drain oil looks great, even though it never dries.)

—Roofing repairs, using the same substances as used on driveways,

—Tree trimming and pruning,

—Tuckpointing,

—Repairing leaking foundations, using sealant or drain oil again,

—Electrical or plumbing work,

—Pumping out septic tanks,

—Exterminating insects. Gypsies have been known to sneak in pieces of termite-infested wood to show to the homeowner/victim.

Fees on all these scams are negotiated and are generally whatever the Gypsy feels he can get from the victim. Sometimes, while working one of these cons, the Gypsies will take advantage of the opportunity to commit a burglary or theft, (see later section).

Auto Body Repairs

This scam works like this: A male Gypsy will drive around town until he locates a damaged vehicle parked in a driveway. Then he'll approach the owner with an offer to make the repairs for a reasonable fee.

After the work is completed, the Gypsy will return to the owner, explaining that the job was much more difficult and time-consuming than he thought and the fee will be much higher.

If the owner accepts the story, the Gypsy takes the money and leaves. If the owner puts up any kind of an argument, the Gypsy will threaten to call the police or initiate some legal action. The owner may become frightened and pay the fee.

If all these tactics fail, Gypsies have been known to replace all the dents in the vehicle, restoring it to its "original" condition.

Burglaries, Thefts

Gypsies frequently use photo ID cards to gain entry to a victim's home. They have been known to pose as repairmen, utility workers, inspectors of various kinds or investigators.

Once inside, they will do any number of things depending on how they (mis)represented themselves. If they entered as plumbing inspectors, for example, they may ask the victim to go into the basement and run water while they check the water meter upstairs or outside. Instead, with the homeowner occupied, they'll commit a theft, or let another offender in to commit the theft or burglary.

They may pretend to be inspectors or surveyors from the city. In this version of the scam, they may have the victim come outside and hold one end of a string so they can check the lot line. Once they're out of sight of the victim, the offenders tie off the string to a tree, fence or other object, hit the house for whatever cash/merchandise they can find, then leave while the victim is still holding the string.

Another scam they use is to say they are there with a refund from a utility company. Once inside, they'll offer the refund in cash, but then discover they don't have the correct change. When the victim goes to make change, they will watch to see where the money is kept or hidden. After the refund is made, one of the offenders will keep the victim busy or distract him with a disturbance of some kind while the other steals the money.

There are as many variations of these scams as there are offenders to work them. Basically, they gain entry through various means like those described above, then commit a theft or burglary, depending on the circumstances. They may also commit a burglary by entering the home of an elderly person who they've observed sitting outside. These cons are closely allied with home repair scams and have been worked at the same time.

Home Invasions

This one isn't even subtle. A group of Gypsies will locate a house with an elderly victim. They will use any excuse necessary to gain entry — like looking for directions or needing a drink of water. Once inside, they will confuse the victim or create a disturbance of some type, even to the point of pushing and shoving the victim or tearing the phone from the wall. While this is taking place, other offenders will be stealing any cash and jewelry they can find.

Hydraulic Jack Repairs

In this case, male Gypsies will enter a gas station, garage or car dealership and ask if any hydraulic jacks need repair. If the dealer offers one, they will pretend to work on it for awhile and then explain that it needs to go into their shop for repairs. Then they'll set a fee for the job and a date for the return of the jack.

It doesn't happen. Once they have the jack, they'll repaint it, make any necessary minor repairs and then resell it to another gas station or garage for $100 to $150.

Sharpening Industrial Tools

Like the hydraulic jack repairs, this one also is worked by the male Gypsies. They will approach a business and explain that they have a method of resizing and sharpening tools. Asking for an old drill bit or gasket punch, they explain that they need to take it with them, but they'll be back in a few days. When they return, they demonstrate by grinding the bit on a bench grinder, then drilling holes in metal with it.

If the victim is convinced that the Gypsies can do what they say and have demonstrated, they will supply them with files, drill bits and other tools. The Gypsies will quote a low price and leave with the items. In a few days, they return again with all the items wrapped up and coated with an oily substance. Then they'll ask for payment. If payment is refused or to be billed, they'll accept part payment or whatever they can get at the moment. The tools they're returning have not been sharpened or cleaned, simply coated with oil and wrapped.

X-ray Film Thefts

Gypsies recognize that X-ray films are valuable for their silver content. For that reason, they steal them. Several methods are used. They will approach a doctor, nurse or hospital employee, either at a doctor's office, clinic or hospital.

They will offer to buy all used X-ray film at a good price. If the offer is accepted, the Gypsies will bring in their own scale and pay by the pound. At this point, the con goes several ways. The scale will weigh light and the Gypsies will pay less for what they are really obtaining.

Or, the Gypsies will say that the silver content is too low and offer a lower price. Another ploy is to locate the new X-ray film supply and simply switch the old for the new. When all else fails, they simply issue bad checks for payment.

Till Dipping

This one is generally worked by three female Gypsies. They will get in line at a store and as they get close to the cash register, one and sometimes more will start some kind of disturbance by asking other people in line unusual questions about the store or its products. They will talk loudly, holding things up while they carry on. With this in progress, one of the other Gypsies will wait for the cash drawer to open. Timing is the key to this scam. While the cashier is misdirected by the disturbance and looks away, the Gypsy will reach into the cash drawer, grabbing whatever she can get. All three then leave the store as quickly as possible, still keeping up the disturbance as they exit.

Cash Thefts from Store Safes

As in the till dipping example, a distraction is used to get to the area where the safe is located. Several Gypsy women will be in the store and get as many clerks and employees as possible distracted by asking for products, complaining or arguing among themselves. Once they have gotten the manager away from the office where the safe is located, one will enter the area and take whatever cash she can grab from the safe or cash drawer. Others will physically block the aisles to prevent anyone from getting too close while the actual theft is in progress. Once the theft is accomplished and the one who has the money leaves the store, the others follow.

Welfare Fraud

Gypsies often apply for any kind of welfare available. They may collect welfare funds from different counties and states under many different names.

Oriental Rug Sales

In reality, this is a burglary in progress. Two male Gypsies will approach a victim at his or her home and attempt to sell an Oriental rug. If the victim is interested, they will unload it from their truck and allow the individual to view it outside. To increase the victim's interest, they offer to put it in the home so the person can see how it looks on the floor.

As they carry the rug into the house, a third Gypsy will hide behind the rug and, once inside, will seek out and steal money or jewelry.

If the homeowner agrees to buy the rug, they will sneak the third Gypsy out in some manner. If the homeowner decides not to buy, the Gypsy goes out the door behind the rug again.

Shoplifting

Certain Gypsies are known to be shoplifters and steal at every opportunity. They use the common methods already discussed, as well as "customize" the scam with Gypsy tactics, like distracting employees or causing disturbances so other Gypsies can do the shoplifting.

One retailer who manages a womens' clothing store in a busy Chicago shopping mall, related that anytime someone comes into her store who even looks like a Gypsy will get the personal and undivided attention of a clerk during her entire time in the store. The clerks, she adds, even assist in the dressing room. She refuses checks, credit cards, exchanges and refunds from Gypsies. Sharp lady.

Oak Tree Sales

In this homeowners' scam, Gypsies will drive around selected neighborhoods and offer to sell residents young oak trees at a reasonable price. Once the deal is made, or sometimes in advance of the sale as a selling point, the Gypsies explain that they'll even plant the tree at no charge. After planting the tree and collecting their fee, the Gypsies leave. Several days later the tree dies. Upon examination, homeowners find that the "trees" have no root system and are, in fact, merely branches cut from existing oak trees.

Social Security Physician

Several Gypsies will select an elderly victim for this one, explaining that they are from the Social Security Administration. They will explain that they have come to check on the victim because he/she may be eligible for additional Social Security or Medicaid benefits. While one pretends to be the doctor and do an examination (?), the other will steal all the money and jewelry they can find in the house.

Fortune Telling

When one thinks of Gypsy crimes and activities, fortune telling always comes to mind. And it's all true. The methods they use have been covered in the chapter on fortune tellers and mediums.

Other Crimes

Many of the cons, scams, thefts and burglaries discussed here are similar in many ways. Some are just variations of others. And today's Gypsies are branching out into other lucrative areas, like drug sales, credit card fraud, bad check writing and other crimes.

Comments by Walstad:

You will find dealing with Gypsies to be an unusual and educational experience. Here are some recommendations that I have compiled from various sources.

1. Good Friday is an active day for Gypsy crimes, so be especially alert.

2. When visiting or working an area, Gypsies will often contact other (Gypsy) fortune tellers. They can be a good source of intelligence information.

3. If you run across a Gypsy wedding or funeral, gather as much information as possible at the time. Most likely you will have Gypsies from all over the country in your area.

4. Maintain a file of Gypsies, recording dates, times, places and types of crimes committed. It may help you to prosecute Gypsy activity.

5. When responding to Gypsy-related calls, gather all possible information on vehicles, offenders and the M.O. Don't overlook anything.

6. Male Gypsies enjoy drinking and gambling and can be a good source of intelligence information.

7. Accommodations at moderately priced, clean and well-known motel chains are known to be preferred for many travelling Gypsies. If Gypsy crimes occur in your area, keep this in mind.

8. When you detect Gypsy activity in your area, notify other nearby police departments with information on vehicles, offenders and their M.O.

9. If you have a bar or restaurant in your area that Gypsies frequent, be sure to maintain some sort of regular surveillance. Maintain records of vehicles and registration information, and let other jurisdictions know that you have this information available.

10. Good sound police work, including checking for proper registration and licenses at traffic stops, will discourage Gypsies from hanging around your area.

If you have made an arrest with Gypsy offenders, here are some recommendations:

1. Because some Gypsies commit so many crimes, it is often difficult for them to recall particular incidents or locations. You'll find it helpful to describe in detail to them the house, circumstances or other information.

2. Try to identify the person or persons making bail for the offender.

3. While in your custody, do your best to keep the Gypsies separated.

4. Do not overlook any children, since they may be concealing the fruits of the crime and the evidence you need.

5. Record all vehicle information from the offender's vehicle(s).

6. Do your best to make positive ID on the offenders. I recognize that it may not be an easy task. Fingerprint checks, tattoos, scars and other identifying marks may be your only means.

7. Photograph and fingerprint all suspects.

8. If the crime merits a bail or bond hearing, do your best to inform the prosecutor about Gypsies and their activities, and hope for a high bail.

9. Gypsies pride themselves on being great liars, and enjoy it. Remember also that Gypsies do not respect the police or have high regard for the criminal justice system.

10. Use the information in this chapter to your advantage; it may give you the edge you need. And remember: patience is a virtue.

> *"Carnival: a collection of rides, games, shows and concessions. In its most primitive form, a merry-go-round and a couple of grind stores might be said to constitute a carnival, but it would be a pretty sorry one."*
>
> —**William Lindsay Gresham**
> *Nightmare Alley*

Carny Knowledge

"...and the real tipoff to a crooked carnival game is when the operator has a hole in the front of his shirt."

This comment came at the end of an interview Walstad conducted with an ex-carny. "It's an old inside carny joke," he continued, "about someone running a 'belly joint.' The operator pushes on the gaff so often, it wears holes in his shirts."

Depending on where you live, as soon as warm weather arrives, so do carnivals, crooked games and all. Carnivals generally follow the sun, staying in the south during the winter months. Throughout the midwest and in the northern states, carnivals start popping up in May.

Carnivals are being hurt by the big amusement and theme parks that are being built throughout the country in or near major metropolitan areas. Accordingly, carnivals are being forced to cut down their routes and move to smaller towns and more rural areas.

Carnivals are like people: no two are the same. Some have no crooked games, some have a few, others have many. Carnival people, or carnies, have their own slang and terminology, just as people in businesses and professions do.

A good example is the term "belly joint." A belly joint is a carnival game that is gaffed and controlled by the operator by leaning his belly again a gaff or mechanical control to determine the outcome of a game.

Here is a list of the most common carnival slang:

Agent — The operator of any carnival game.

Alibi agent — The operator of any crooked carnival game where the operator gives advice to the player about what s/he is doing wrong.

Alibi store — A crooked carnival game, often a game of skill (?) that the player cannot win, and the operator offers advice to the player of what s/he is doing wrong.

Burn the lot — To cheat the players so badly that it will make it next to impossible for another carnival to come into that area for a long time.

Count store — A crooked carnival game where the player accumulates points through a game in order to win a prize.

Flat store — Any crooked carnival game.

Flattie — The operator of any crooked carnival game.

Grind joint — A carnival game, usually crooked because — although the player just keeps missing winning it all — it is almost impossible to win, and the player grinds away at his money.

G-wheel or G-joint — Any wheel or spindle game that is gaffed, ('G' stands for gaffed).

Hanky-Pank — Usually a straight carnival game where the prizes the players win usually cost less than the cost to play.

Joint — Any carnival game, straight or crooked.

PC game, or **percentage game** — Any carnival game where the odds are in favor of the house winning. (Las Vegas-type odds.)

Peek store — A crooked carnival game where the player, through some sort of game play, selects a numbered object that designates a prize. The operator either peeks at the number himself, or shows the number to the player but covers part of the digit to make it appear to be another number.

Store — A carnival game, straight or crooked.

HOW A **PEEK STORE** CAN OPERATE CROOKED...

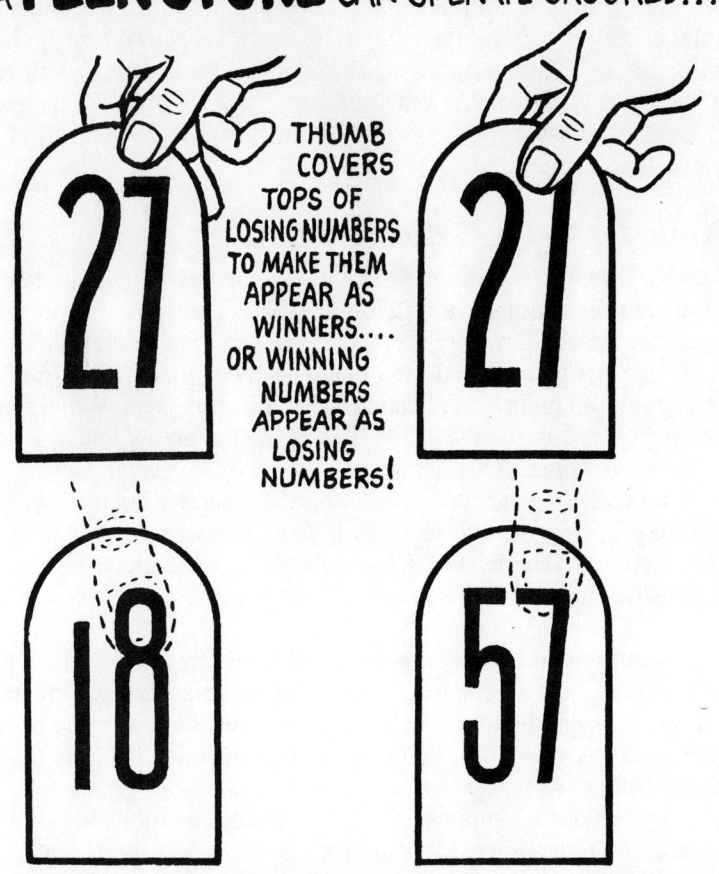

THUMB COVERS TOPS OF LOSING NUMBERS TO MAKE THEM APPEAR AS WINNERS.... OR WINNING NUMBERS APPEAR AS LOSING NUMBERS!

BY HOLDING THE TAG RIGHT SIDE UP, IT SHOWS 191

BY HOLDING THE TAG UPSIDE DOWN, IT SHOWS 161

Carnival Games

Here are some of the most popular carnival games in use today, categorized by those that are almost always crooked, those that are sometimes gaffed, and those that are generally honest. If you run across a game not specifically mentioned here, look carefully at the game, how it works and what the operator is doing. You'll probably find a similar game listed here.

Almost Always Gaffed Games

G-Wheels or **Spindles** — This is a game that looks like a wheel of fortune laid out on a horizontal table. The game has a spindle that spins an attached arrow. The spindle is centered in a circle made up of nails or pegs pounded into the board. Between each of the nails or pegs is a color or marker, indicating what prize is won if the arrow stops between those particular nails. The tip of the arrow touches each of the nails as it spins. This game can be gaffed several ways. The most popular is the mechanical spindle that the operator controls with a hidden button, causing the wheel to stop only between certain nails or pegs. (Co-author Walstad has such a wheel in his collection, and it never misses during demonstrations.)

Count or **Razzle Games** — Games where the player is playing to accumulate points that lead to a winning prize is a count game, also known as a grind game. Usually these games have a razzle board posted that converts their play into points. The operator controls the game by miscounting.

For example, suppose the game is called 'football.' The object is to score a touchdown by rolling eight dice. The numbers on the dice are totalled and, by using the razzle chart, the number indicates how many yards the ball can be advanced. If the numbers on the eight dice totalled 33, for example, the razzle chart would indicate that you could move the ball one yard on the playing board. If you rolled a 44, you would move ahead 20 yards.

The operator controls the game by miscounting the total on the dice. On the first play, he will usually miscount to give a good score that will advance the ball 10 to 20 yards. Each play costs more money. As the player slowly advances the ball, just as he's ready to quit, he picks up some more big yards. Once again, the operator has miscounted to keep the player in the game.

The player never makes the necessary points to win the big prize, which is usually a TV, VCR, stereo system or microwave oven. The odds of rolling a total of eight or 48 using eight dice (to get a touchdown in one play) are one in 1,679,616.

There are many variations of this game. Also, once the player has gotten into the game, the operator may offer a cash prize instead of the merchandise. The operator also will try to keep the player isolated from others while the game is in play so no one can wise him up. Experienced

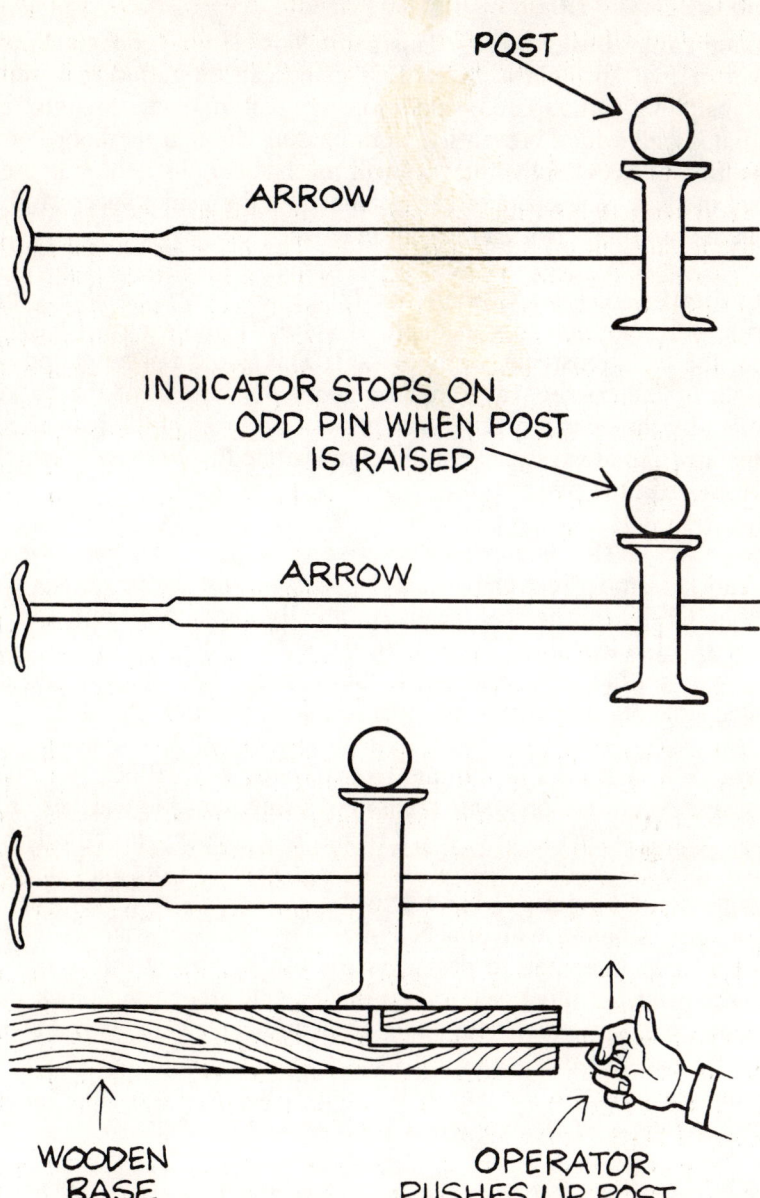

operators of this game know just how far they can string a particular player along.

Often Gaffed Games

Long-range Basketball — This game looks simple enough. Shoot a basket or two and win a prize. This game can be gaffed in several ways, including a hoop too small for the ball to pass through, an overinflated ball which prevents it from passing through the hoop, or a combination of both. Sometimes a small mechanical obstruction is used to block the ball. The operator can demonstrate the game (successfully) with an underinflated ball and lots of practice.

Bushel Baskets — Another easy (?) game. This is an alibi game requiring only that you toss a couple of softballs into a bushel basket. To win, the balls must stay in the basket. This game can be gaffed by the angle of the baskets, a drumhead under the bottom of the basket controlled by the operator, or by the softness/hardness of the balls used. The operator can always successfully demonstrate this because his angle is different than the player's.

Six Cat — This is another deceptive alibi game. All you have to do is knock a stuffed cat or two off the shelf to win the prize. Six Cat can be gaffed by mechanical means (in a belly joint) to make the shelf the cats sit on adjustable. By making the shelf wider, it is impossible for the cat to fall from the shelf. Sometimes the cats are heavily weighted, making it nearly impossible to knock them off the shelf.

Watch a la Blocks — "In the Evans Watch A La Block, we offer the concessionaire the only safe method of using valuable watches on a hoop la stand." That's how W.C. Evans & Company described this game in their 1918-1919 catalog of carnival games. Does that suggest this game could be gaffed? For a fee, the player gets to toss a ring or rings at various blocks with attached prizes; in this case, watches. Gaffs include a hoop too small to pass over the block, a mechanical gaff to slightly expand the block size or a piece of felt around the block that can be bunched up to block the hoop. Even an honest game is just about impossible because the hoops just barely encircle the block. From the angle the player tosses the hoops, it's almost impossible. Similar types of block games offer stuffed animals, radios and other prizes.

Knife or **Cane Rack** — The object is to toss a small hoop over the head of a special knife or cane handle. The handles have movable heads, allowing the hoop to pass over in one position, but not in another. The angle of the operator, different from that of the player, allows him to demonstrate this successfully.

Ring Over the Bottle — Similar to the Knife Rack, except that you toss a ring over a pop bottle. This can be gaffed by using small

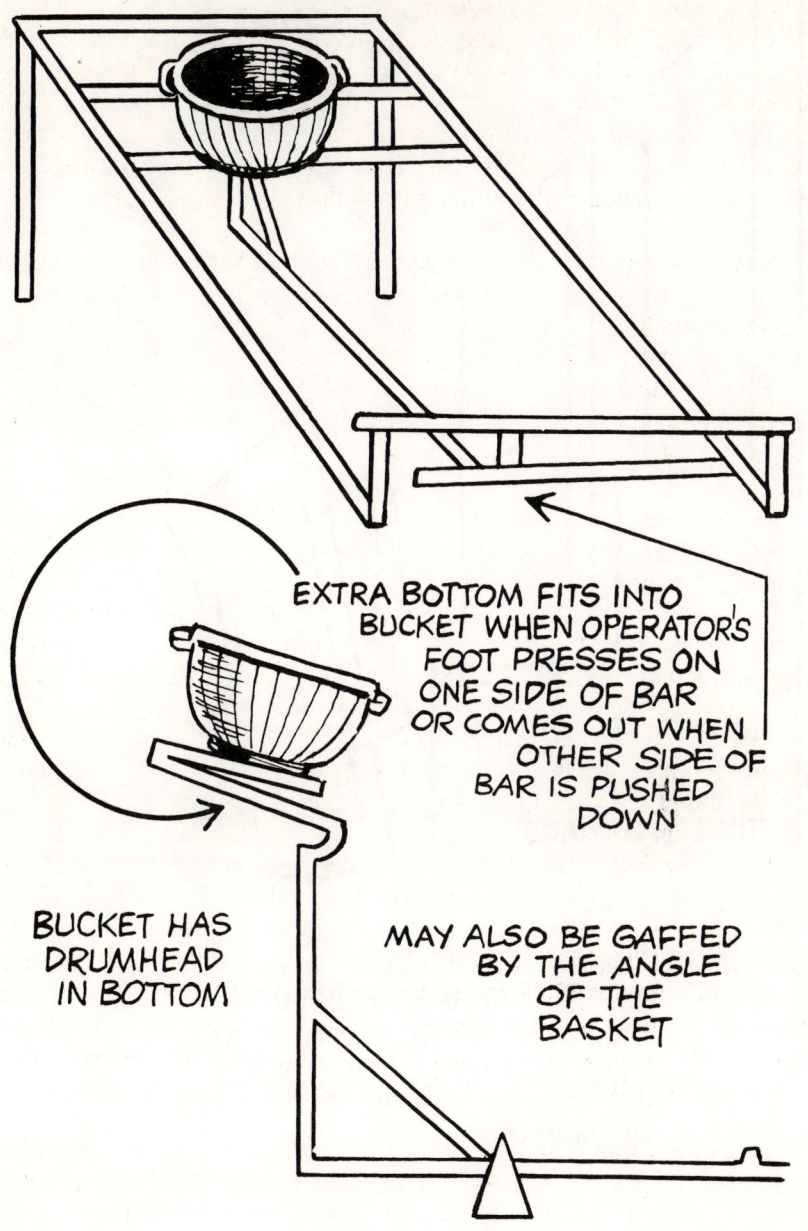

HOW **BLOCK GAMES** ARE GAFFED...

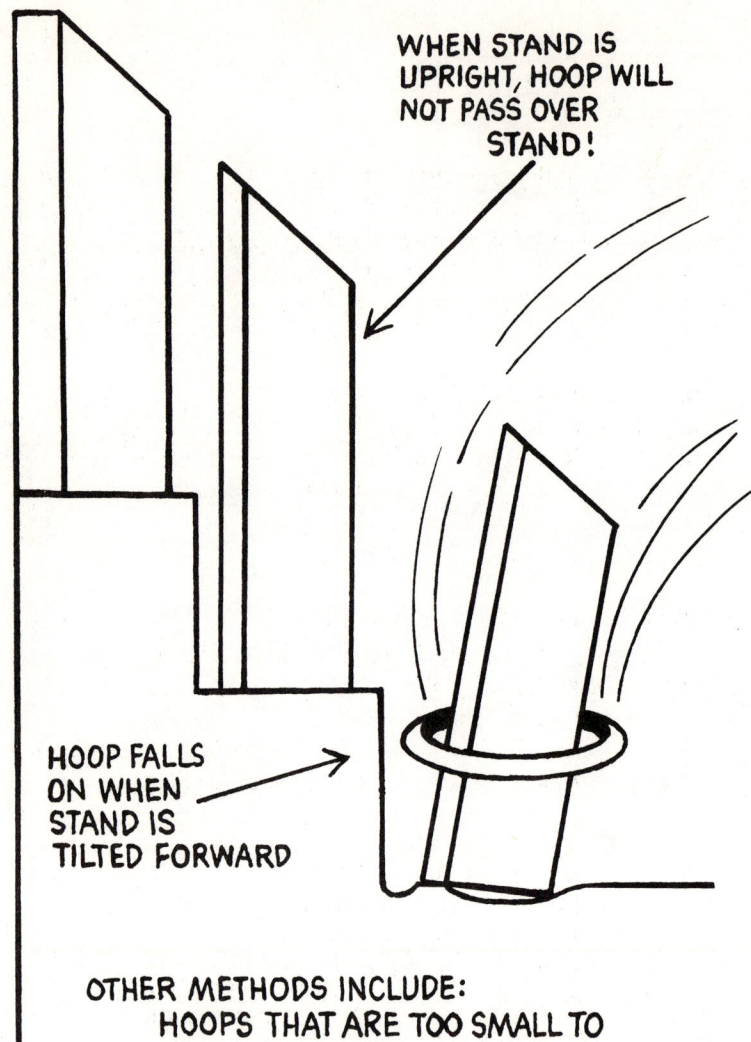

WHEN STAND IS UPRIGHT, HOOP WILL NOT PASS OVER STAND!

HOOP FALLS ON WHEN STAND IS TILTED FORWARD

OTHER METHODS INCLUDE:
HOOPS THAT ARE TOO SMALL TO PASS OVER STAND, AND THE FELT, COVERING THE STAND, IS BUNCHED UP... PREVENTING THE HOOP FROM PASSING OVER.

rings, or by using a small, clear piece of glue or similar substance on the bottle to prevent the ring from passing over.

One Ball — An alibi game where the player attempts to knock three metal bottles off a table. This can be gaffed by using a weighted bottle or bottles. If one or more heavy bottles are used, they are placed on the bottom of the stack. Some states have laws regarding the allowed weight of the bottles used.

Nail Joint — Another alibi game where the player attempts to drive one or more nails into a piece of wood with only one hit of the hammer. This game always draws the do-it-yourself experts and carpenters. This can be gaffed by using two sets of nails. One type consists of regular nails, a second set is a softer nail that will bend easily. Both types of nails are held, separately, in an apron worn by the operator.

Shooting Gallery — There are many different types of shooting galleries, ranging from cork guns to BB guns to .22 caliber to fully automatic BB guns. The most common ways to gaff these games are with inaccurate sights (bent), weighted targets (cans), impossible targets (can will not fall, even if hit) and almost impossible targets (requiring the player to completely shoot out the red star).

Plate Pitch — Is this game gaffed or not? Yes and no. In this case, the gaff is right in front of you. The game works like this: you pitch coins at plates in an attempt to have the coin not only land on, but stay on, a plate. Here's the gaff. The prizes offered — usually very large stuffed animals — are hung right above the plates. This makes it impossible for the player to get the right angle so the coin will stay on the plate.

Swinger — An alibi game where the player swings a ball attached to a chain or string past a bowling pin in an effort to knock the pin down on the backswing, as the ball returns. When the game is gaffed, by offsetting the pin slightly, it is impossible to hit the pin. This can be observed in some cases by a pin or small nail protruding from the playing board, and two small holes in the bottom of the bowling pin. If the pin is placed in one hole, the bowling pin can be hit (for demonstration purposes). When placed in the other hole, the ball cannot hit the pin.

Dart Toss — There are many variations of dart games. The player usually tosses one or more darts at a target, balloons, colored circles or something similar. Some of the dart games are not gaffed, and are purely percentage or grind games (hit a red dot or circle and win a prize). Some are of the "peek" variety. A game where you hit the target and the operator turns over and looks at a tag that tells you your prize is a peek game.

Three Pin — This is a grind game where the player rolls a ball down an alley (of sorts) in an attempt to knock down three pins. This game can be gaffed by the placement of the pins.

String Game — A grind game where the player pulls on a string from a bundle (usually 72), and wins the prize attached to it, or a number which corresponds to a prize. This can be worked as a peek game when using numbers, or it can be gaffed by the operator who folds back, or cuts short, the strings attached to the major prizes.

Bowling Ball Roll — A unique game that is usually coin-operated, allowing the operator to watch over several games at one time. The object is to roll a bowling ball on a track over a hill and into a valley, attempting to keep the ball in the valley. It can be gaffed by the tilt of the table, which is controlled by adjustable legs.

Spot the Spot — A grind game where the player drops five disks onto the table playing area, attempting to completely cover a large circle. The game is almost impossible because the player has to drop the disks from several inches above the table and must completely cover the circle or spot. It can be gaffed by the use of disks too small to cover the spot. The operator can successfully demonstrate an ungaffed game by just plain practice and experience, or a gaffed game by using one of his disks which is slightly larger than those the player uses.

Pop It In — An alibi game where the player tosses baseballs into a box with many square compartments. The object is to get the ball to stay in one of the compartments. This game can be gaffed by the angle of the box with the compartments. The steeper the angle, the less likely that the ball will stay in.

Clothes Line — A peek game where the player tosses rings in an attempt to get a ring over a clothespin. After the pin is ringed, the operator looks at or shows a number (on the back of the clothespin) to the player, which corresponds to a prize.

English Pool — An alibi game where the player hits a cue ball into another ball that has a coin resting on it. The object is to knock the coin out of a small circle drawn around the ball. It is almost impossible to do. It can be demonstrated by the operator by slightly offsetting the coin when balanced on the ball.

Huckly Buck — An alibi game where the player tosses baseballs into wooden kegs. This is similar to the Bushel Basket Game and Pop It In. The game is gaffed by the angle at which the kegs are set and the hardness/softness of the balls.

HOW THE **STRING** GAME IS GAFFED

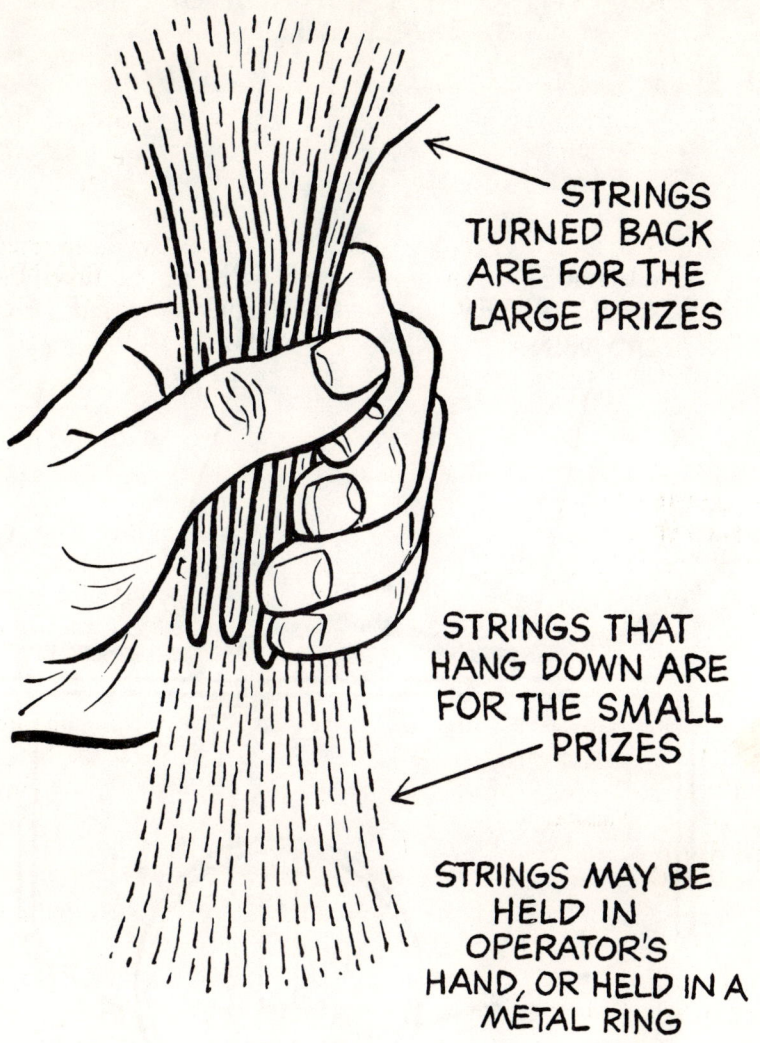

STRINGS TURNED BACK ARE FOR THE LARGE PRIZES

STRINGS THAT HANG DOWN ARE FOR THE SMALL PRIZES

STRINGS MAY BE HELD IN OPERATOR'S HAND, OR HELD IN A METAL RING

MAY ALSO BE GAFFED BY CUTTING THE STRINGS SHORT FOR THE LARGE PRIZES.

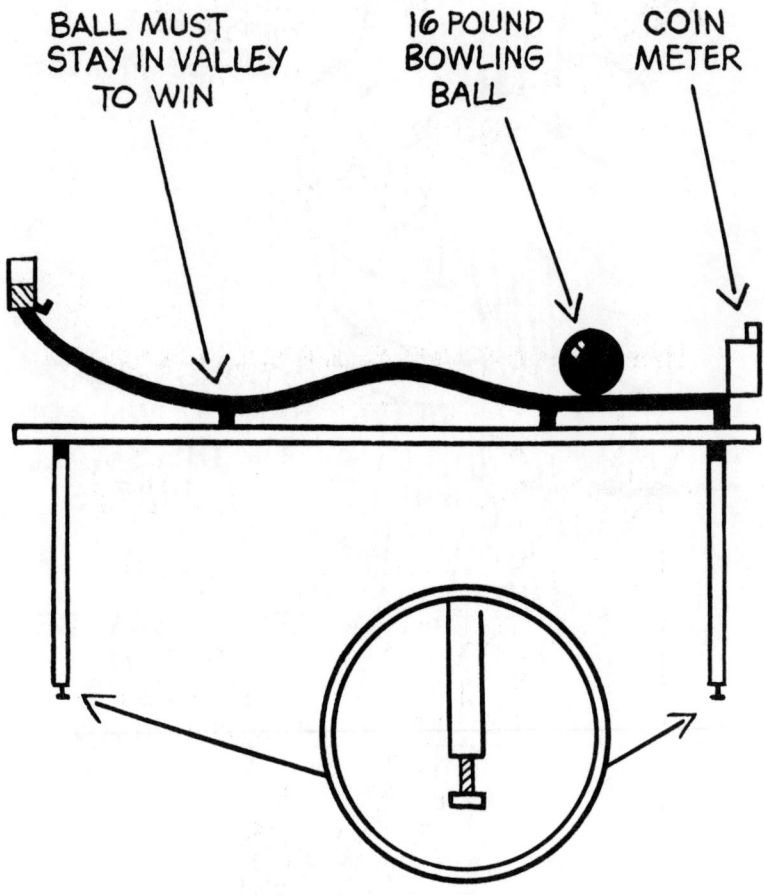

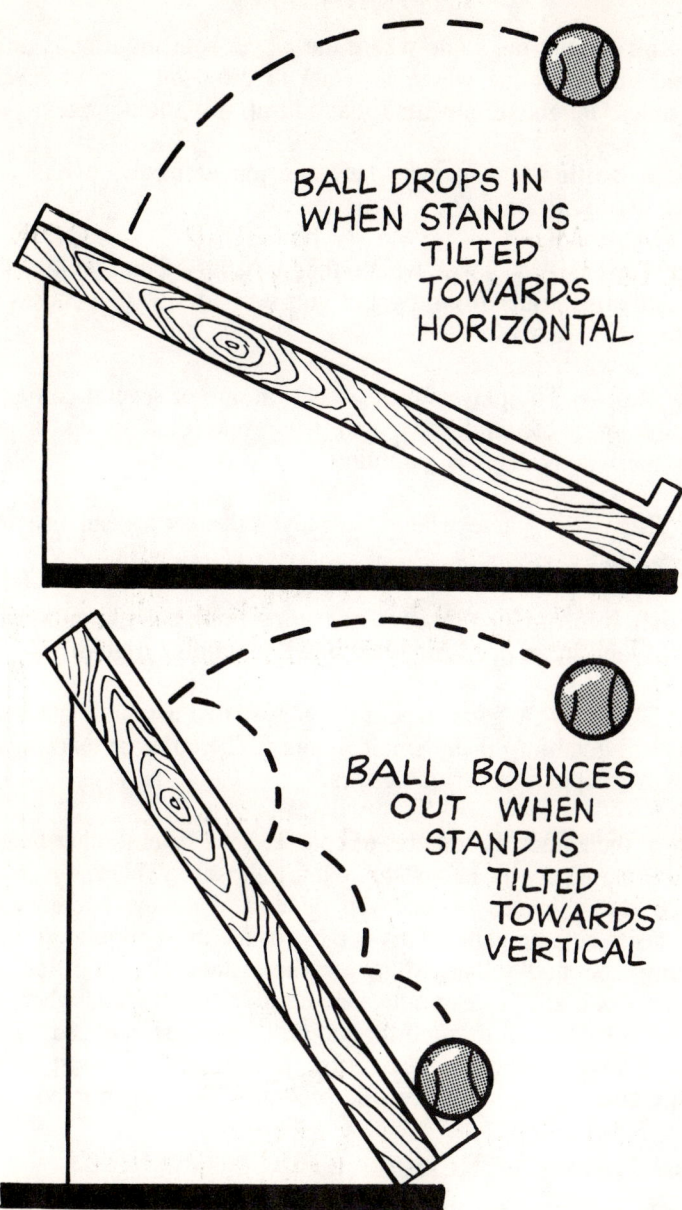

Games Usually Not Gaffed

Break a Plate or Record — An alibi percentage game where the player throws a ball in an attempt to break or chip two plates or records that are placed close together.

Skee Ball — A grind game where the player rolls eight balls down an alley and up an incline where they are to drop into one of several numbered holes. Points are awarded that add up to various prizes.

Break a Bottle — A game where the player throws a ball at a bottle in an attempt to break it.

Water Race — A game where the players attempt to break a balloon by shooting water from a water gun into a target that causes air to flow into the balloon.

Crazy Ball — The player places a bet on one of several colors. A large multi-colored die is tossed, and whatever color shows on top determines the winner. This is gambling.

Bean Bag — A game where the player throws a bean bag at a stack of pop cans.

Goldfish Joint — The player tosses ping pong balls in an attempt to get one to land in an open-mouthed bowl containing a goldfish.

Penny Pitch — A game where the player tosses coins onto a flat board that is divided into many small squares. The color or markings in the squares correspond to various prizes.

Many of the games listed here, of course, have several other names. Often, the operator will name the game himself. There are many variations of these games as well, all dependent on the operator and how he wants to run the game. This is a list of the most popular carnival games being operated today. Many of the games are modified and become one-of-a-kind. For example, one carnival has a game where the player tosses a basketball through the mouth of a monster's head, which had been cut from plywood and painted. It's an obvious twist on the Basketball Game and, if gaffed, would probably use over-inflated balls.

Carnival Games in Review

1. Keep in mind that most carnival games can be played either straight or crooked (a two-way store),

2. There is a good chance that just about any wheel-type game is going to be gaffed,

3. Games that use point conversion charts are usually crooked (a razzle game),

4. Any game where the operator looks at a number selected by the player could be run as a peek game,

5. An operator will often offer cash to the player, instead of a prize,

6. Many carnival games constitute illegal gambling (depending on state and local laws),

7. Inspect all games carefully.

Conversation with a carny

Carnies seldom "tip" the inside information they have to outsiders. Several years ago, however, co-author Walstad had two interviews with an ex-carny. Here is his summation of those interviews.

This ex-carny is still involved in the business, although he does not travel any more. He wishes to remain anonymous, and his wishes will be respected. In fact, he stated that if other carnies knew he was giving away this kind of information, he would be in for, as he put it, "big trouble," possibly violent in nature. I had to assure him several times that his name would not be used.

With that assurance, he continued.

Every carnival is different, he told me. It all depends on the owner and what he will allow or will not allow to occur on his lot.

Crooked carnival games, he says, are still being built today. He said that if you were to call a carnival game manufacturer who knew you (as running crooked or straight games), they will tell you right on the phone if a particular game is for you or not, referring to whether it is crooked or straight.

Crooked carnivals, he explained, run an average of 25 percent crooked games — sometimes more, sometimes less. He added that crooked carnival operators love to play state and county fairs because no one seems to care if the games are crooked or not.

My carny confidant added an interesting point here. He said that almost all carnivals will play it super straight when working dates near their home base. "Too close to home," he said.

Game operators or agents work on a daily flat fee or pay a percentage of their gross to the carnival owner for the privilege of working with the carnival. If an operator gets caught skimming funds or holding out on the owner, he will be blackballed and find work hard to get.

He joked about how stupid some of the "marks" could be and said that often, after closing, the carnies would all sit around, swap stories and laugh about their best mark of the day. Incidentally, the term "mark" comes from early carnival history. If one operator found a "live one," he would mark the back of the person's coat or shirt with chalk so that other game operators could spot him.

My confidant confirmed some of the unusual values and principles that exist among carnies. For example, he said that if a carnival had overbooked and was unable to provide the necessary rides and attractions to fill a date, no other carnival would even think of helping them out — even if they had a whole carnival sitting idle with no date to play.

However, he added that if a carnival met with an act of God, fire, tornado or other natural disaster, any carnival near or far would lend a hand with manpower, money, equipment loans, rides, concessions and games.

Almost all of the carnies he knew did not use their real names but, instead, used an alias. He knew as a fact that some were running from the law, which explains one reason for an alias. Is there a way, I asked him, to track any of these people down or determine who's who? He said that there is an organization called The Showmen League of America, similar to other fraternal groups, to which most carnies belong. It could provide a starting point.

Gypsies often travel with carnivals, he said. Several years ago, the Gypsies he knew were part of the "John's clan," to his knowledge, the biggest Gypsy clan involved with carnivals. They ran things like guess your weight, handwriting analysis, the duck pond and fortune-telling booths.

I asked him what, in his opinion, was the best way to deal with carnivals. He said, "Talk to them in their own language. Let them know you are knowledgeable about crooked carnival games and how they work." He said that if you are firm and demand that the letter of the law be followed, this would do much to keep crooked carnivals out of your area. He said that carnivals do communicate with each other and that once an area is known for demanding a clean lot, the word spreads. In closing, he said that carnivals are changing like everything else. Drugs are available, and are being used by some of the younger carnies, a fact that I could tell really bothered him. It was a nostalgic interview for him. I sensed that he was glad to be out of active carnival life but, at the same time, I could tell that he missed it also. Carnivals are like that.

Comments by Walstad:

Speak to carnies in their own language; let them know you understand their games and how they work. Have your local health, electrical and building inspectors check all concessions and rides. Inspect all games carefully, checking out the props for unusual mechanics. Try the games to see if they work. After the carnival has opened, come back and make a follow-up inspection since the props you examined earlier are sometimes switched for gaffed props later, even though the games appear to be working the same way.

Check for the proper licenses, permits and required insurance papers. Often, smaller carnivals will try to avoid the costs of licenses and permits.

Increase your surveillance on the last day the carnival is in your area. Burning the lot on the last day is a common practice.

Speak with the agent/owner/manager and explain that you will not tolerate any crooked games, shortchanging or other scams. Let the individual know that you will have plainclothes officers on the lot from time to time, watching and playing the games. Ask the person how many uniformed officers he or she would like to hire for security. A straight carnival likes the police around, a crooked one does not.

At the first sign of any crooked games in use, make arrests if possible, and reevaluate the carnival's license to operate.

If the carnival is being sponsored by a local church or civic group, be sure to speak with the people in charge and advise them of the crooked games and scams that can occur. The owner/agent will listen to them as much, if not more so, than he will listen to the police.

A few years ago, a fellow officer in my department told me that his father used to supply the prizes and tear-open tickets to locally sponsored carnivals for their jar games.

He explained to me that when they received the boxes of tickets, the winning tickets would be in a separate bag. Then, the winning tickets would not be added to the others until the carnival had been running a few days, then added slowly as the days progressed. So I suggest that if you're going to play jar games, wait until the end of the carnival's run.

Just one more thing: Watch for game operators with holes in their shirts!

> *"Let him that hath understanding count the number of the beast: for it is the number of a man; and his number is six hundred threescore and six."*
>
> —*Revelation 13:18*

Twisting Satan's Tail: Cults and crimes in the world of darkness

Satanism. Devil worship. '666.' The mark of the beast.

Are satanic cults real? Are satanic cults in your area? Are people in satanic cults committing crimes? Unfortunately, the answer to all three questions is 'yes.'

Estimates are that there are more than one million satanists in this country. The majority of them are linked in a highly organized, secret network of cults. They are not limited to large cities, they exist in small towns as well. If you start paying closer attention to the graffiti on building walls, you'll see the evidence. Have you ever seen the numbers '666' or the letters 'FFF?' These are the signs of the devil used by satanic worshippers to spread the word of the devil.

The numbers '6' for example, or '666,' represent the Biblical number of the Beast. The letter 'F' is used because it represents the sixth letter of the alphabet. Occasionally, other numbers are used, usually multiples of '6,' like '18,' the sum of the numbers '666.'

Even more chilling is the fact that evidence we commonly see is not displayed by "upper-level satanists." Only the less sophisticated satanists "advertise" and leave a trail. The worst crimes and victimizations are perpetrated by men and women who seldom leave evidence and who blend easily with the mainstream of our communities.

Satanic symbols turn up on heavy metal "music" (we use the term loosely) album covers, along with pentagrams and devil's horns. Don't just look at the album covers though, listen to the words. You'll be shocked.

Visit your local bookstore and check out how many book titles deal with satanism, the devil or the occult. Check out video themes.

Next time you're in a gift shop, look at some of the jewelry with satanic themes and symbols available for sale. For whatever reason, satanism is a popular subject these days. More than a passing fad however, satanism is a serious problem.

Satanic cults are involved in more crimes than you might suspect. The crimes range from minor thefts and vandalism to ritualized abuse of children, rape, mayhem and murder. Most, because of their bizarre nature, leave victims and their families in a state of mental anguish, and challenge skeptical police officials to accept reports which are beyond the limits of their training and experience. There are endless horror stories about victims of satanic cults. This is not the place to relate those incidents. Quite possibly, you've already been involved in investigating satanic cult-originated crimes.

Satanic cults in a con game book?

The authors debated about whether or not to include information about satanic cults in this book. Technically, it's not a con game. In reality, it is one of the most serious. Satanic cults are conning the minds of young people in this country.

Their success at remaining hidden for decades in our society is due largely to their deft use of illusion, double-meaning, deception and diversion.

Also, much of the material presented in this book tends to overlap in one way or another. It's what artists and painters refer to as the "wet edge" — one thing leads to another.

Example: Anton LaVey, author of *The Satanic Bible,* is a former lion tamer and palm reader.

Consider how a cult might recruit a new member. Assume that you're a fraudulent medium, fortune teller or spiritualist. You're also a member of a satanic cult. Here comes a troubled man or woman who spills out his or her life story. This individual already has a predisposition to occult influence because he is consulting you.

You learn about the person, family, friends, work habits and problems. You learn about illnesses, weaknesses, drug or alcohol problems. You learn that the person is alone, with no family or friends. In time, you'll locate the perfect individual who would be receptive to joining a cult, or becoming the victim of some sick cult crime.

Prime candidates are those who have (temporarily or permanently) lost their stabilizing structure/support mechanisms and are susceptible to anything that comes along. Teens, recent widows and divorcees, recruits in boot camp, prisoners and college freshmen are all high-potential targets for recruitment.

It has only been within the past few years that law enforcement has been openly acknowledging satanic cults and their involvement in crimes.

One possible reason for this was expressed on the popular ABC Newsmagazine, *20/20*, produced by ABC News. A fascinating yet disturbing segment of their television documentary, which aired May 16, 1985, was titled "The Devil Worshippers."

During the program, Tom Jarriel, ABC News correspondent, was asked why there wasn't more police involvement.

His response was that police were reluctant to investigate these incidents as satanic crimes. He stated that communities were reluctant to have their reputations stigmatized as the home of the devil. "They prefer to try to categorize them as drug-related crimes, sex-related crimes or robbery or something that they're more familiar with," he said.

Also, prosecution is much harder if satanic influences are mentioned — even good cases are lost because the prosecution didn't lay sufficient groundwork, or the judge/jury just wouldn't/couldn't believe it.

The Maine Supreme Court's decision in the Waterhouse murder case established satanism as an acceptable motive for the first time.

"...We acknowledge that evidence of defendant's satanic beliefs carried with it the potential for creating unfair prejudice. Nevertheless, the evidence was relevant and probative on the issues of both motive and intent..." (Decision No. 4216, Law Docket No. LIN-85-23, Aug. 15, 1986.)

More recently, on the program, *Geraldo*, by the Investigative News Group, hosted by Geraldo Rivera, the subject of "Satanic Cults and Children" was presented Nov. 19, 1987.

Guests on the program included the parents of satanic victims, an ex-satanist, a satanic cult detoxifier, a psychologist and Kurt Jackson, a detective from the Beaumont, Calif., police department who specializes in occult crimes.

Transcripts of the program are available by writing to Journal Graphics Inc., 267 Broadway, New York, NY 10007. (Transcript charges were $3 each, at the time this book went to press.)

Networking support available

Today, many concerned law enforcement officials are helping to educate fellow police officers on the specifics of these crimes. The developing network should be enormously beneficial in tracking down these cult criminals.

It is important that all law enforcement officers be educated on subjects they may become involved with.

A major source of information in this area is Lieutenant Larry Jones of the Boise, Idaho Police Department. Lt. Jones is the president of the board and editor of the *File 18 Newsletter*, published by the private, non-profit Cult Crime Impact Network, Inc. This newsletter serves as a clearing house for current information on cult crimes and occult crime training material across the United States. It is available only to bona fide law enforcement officials and qualified civilians who have entered the fight against cult crime. Write on official department letterhead for more information. (See the Resources section at the back of this book.)

That this can be a dangerous area for investigating officers was emphasized by Jones in an editor's note in the October 1987 issue of *File 18 Newsletter.*

Traditional tools not effective

"My greatest misgiving about working on *File 18* is that we will give you just enough information to be dangerous — to yourselves. Occult crimes and ritual activities carry very real, very heavy spiritual implications along with the physical ones. We expect that you noble, dedicated officers will wade right into the middle of such investigations without a selfish thought.

"However, you may be battling with forces which are impervious to your wrist-twists, your batons or your service firearms — and they may destroy you. These things are unseen to most of us, probably scoffed at or written off as Hollywood/overactive imaginations by the majority. But, in our natural state, we are helpless to defend against unseen enemies; spiritual training and spiritually effective tools are required."

Jones amplified his warning to this book's co-author, Smith, in a letter dated Jan. 29, 1988. He wrote, "When confronted with those criminals who are led or controlled by supernatural, evil beings, philosophies or motivations, traditional police tools are not effective. If a cop is in a head-to-head confrontation with the prince of darkness or his troops, then that cop had better have the 'defeater of Satan' on his side as well as every bit of spiritual armor and assistance available.

"The spiritual warfare aspects are difficult — if not impossible — for many officers to understand or accept; therefore, they can be a stumbling block. Mike Warnke (of Warnke Ministries, Danville, Ky. and an able resource at cult/occult crime scenes) told me that, in his opinion, the Christian police officers were the best prepared to be on the cutting edge in the fight against satanic crimes.

"Also, an officer whose imagination is captured by the occult and who starts to study about or dabble in actual occult activity is just as prone to being enslaved by it as anyone else. The big lures are power, control and instant gratification of lust, money and ego...all the weaknesses of the flesh," Jones wrote.

Satanic cult involvement

Basically, there are three types of individuals who become involved with satanic cults and practices.

1. **Dabblers.** These are self-styled individuals, mostly teens, who fall into this category. Their motto is "Do what you want to do," or "Do your own thing." Signs to look for include involvement with "heavy metal" rock music, experimentation

with drug usage and attitudes reflecting the mottos above. Although this group is not as dangerous as full-fledged cult members, they do practice rituals and have been responsible for many unspeakable crimes.
2. **Devil worshippers.** These are not full-fledged cult members either. Like most cult activists, this group tends to go its own way, but is dangerous enough to cause physical, emotional and spiritual harm to members and victims during their rituals.
3. **Satanic cult members.** These individuals are actively involved with satanic rites and rituals. Members may practice the beliefs in *The Satanic Bible*. Depending on the cult, they may be involved with sex rituals, animal sacrifice, incest, sexual abuse of children and murder. Many signs and symbols will be in evidence at their rituals but, because of the nature of their crimes, they practice much more secrecy and operate "underground."

Satanic secrecy and sickness

Satanic cults thrive on secrecy. Without it, they would cease to exist. Not surprisingly, then, severe steps are taken to ensure their secrecy.

Their codes of secrecy are enforced by blackmail, the threat of exposure to a person's involvement, threats of injury or death to family and friends or threats to their own lives. The more information about satanism that becomes public, the less they like it.

Children play a big part in satanic cult activities because of the innocence of children who are believed to be special to God. Children are used and abused in every possible scenario imaginable (and some unimaginable) during ritualized abuse.

Children are used to recruit other children into the cult, as sexual playthings and as victims of a satanic ritual sacrifice. Even newborn infants (often dedicated for sacrifice by their mothers who are cult members) are victims of ritual infanticide.

Possible indicators of satanic involvement

Satanic cult activities and crimes usually occur in private, secluded areas. If your investigation of a crime leads you into such an area and you discover one or more of the following signs, there is a strong possibility of satanic involvement. Here are some of the clues:

1. The symbols "666" or "FFF" as tattoos, jewelry, marked on clothing or in evidence elsewhere,
2. Pentagrams or crosses,
3. Candles or candle drippings of various colors (which are significant) used during satanic rituals,
4. The use of stolen or vandalized Christian symbols and implements, such as crosses, chalices, holy water, wafers, etc.,
5. Unusual designs or drawings on the ground, floor or walls (pentagrams, for example),

SATANIC SYMBOLS

THE NUMBER "SIX"	HORNS & TAIL ADDED TO LETTER
FFF SIXTH LETTER OF THE ALPHABET **666** SIGN OF THE DEVIL	**NATAS** "SATAN" BACKWARDS
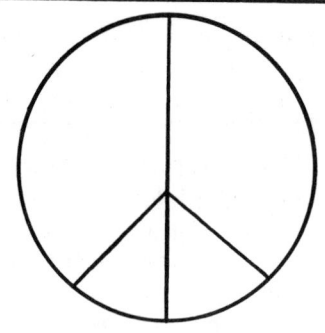 UPSIDE DOWN BROKEN CROSS	 INVERTED PENTAGRAM WITH GOAT'S HEAD

6. Animal mutilations,
7. The use of animal parts (bones, feathers, hair) to make signs and symbols,
8. An absence of blood in dead animals,
9. A makeshift altar with candles, knives, chalices and other ritualistic elements,
10. Voodoo-type dolls with pins in them,
11. Bowls of powder, colored salt or herbs, for use in ceremonies,
12. Human or animal skulls and bones, for decoration and use in ceremonies,
13. Robes, particularly black, white and scarlet, for use in ceremonies,
14. Rooms draped in black or red,
15. Books on satanism, rituals, spells and magick,
16. A goat's head, either real or a drawing,
17. Human or animal cremation,
18. Missing parts from bodies, or human body parts with no body,
19. Unusual location and positioning of bodies,
20. Unusual location of stab wounds or cuts,
21. Branding or burn marks on battery victims or bodies,
22. Signs of blood-letting,
23. The presence of incense on bodies,
24. Signs of cannibalism,
25. Outdoor trail markers, with satanic symbols,
26. Eating feces, drinking blood/urine,
27. Scarring or injection marks inside body openings, such as anus, vagina, eyelids, ears,
28. Strange alphabets, backward writing or numerology,
29. *Book of Shadows* or *Book of Spells,* usually a handwritten book, sometimes in blood,
30. Significant dates upon which crimes occur.

By no means is this a complete list of the clues or evidence that would suggest satanic involvement. You could also come across several of these signs and not have any satanic involvement. Your own investigation will determine what you have. CCIN can help investigators network with others who have already been through such crimes.

During an investigation of child abuse, kidnapping, missing persons or other crimes against an individual, if the victim or witness starts describing torture, bizarre sexual activities, unusual ceremonies or rituals to you, consider the strong possibility of satanic involvement.

Comments by Walstad:

We've included this information because satanic- and occult-related crimes may be linked with fraudulent fortune tellers, spiritualists and mediums. And, as Larry Jones, director of the Cult Crime Impact Network, wrote us: "Perhaps satanism is the biggest 'con' and 'swindle' of them all. It promises total freedom, yet exacts total bondage."

More and more information on this subject is becoming available to law enforcement. I urge you to continue your education in this area by reading as widely as possible on the subject. But note: intense study of resource books and materials by occult sources or practitioners is hazardous. Preferred is studying overviews and synopses by credible authors who have studied the occult traditions. The unknown realm of the occult beckons with many lures. Study and/or experimentation are to be avoided. There are safer ways to test for poisonous chemicals than by tasting them.

Satanic cult members are committing horrible, sickening crimes in the name of the devil. If you uncover satanic crimes in your investigations, classify them as such in your reports. Spread the word.

I have difficulty believing some of the things I have read in my research in this area, particularly those aspects of crimes involving young children.

The people who are involved in satanic cults are sometimes disturbed and deranged individuals who are as sick as their deeds and actions indicate. Others are often as sane as you or I. Their beliefs are as ancient as ours might be, and 180 degrees opposite from the traditional Judeo-Christian experience.

One final word: Use extreme caution if you find yourself confronting cult members. They have everything to lose by being exposed. Go back and re-read Lt. Jones' admonition from the *File 18 Newsletter.*

> *"Something for nothing has ever tempted the simple and unsophisticated; indeed, it is a trait of human nature upon which the swindler everywhere, and in all ages, has relied to his profit."*
>
> —**Harry Houdini**
> *The Right Way To Do Wrong*

Educating the Public: A one-hour community relations presentation

One of the best ways to improve your department's image with the public is through face-to-face programs and community relations activities.

Most police departments in major metropolitan areas have community relations officers assigned to this function. Departments in smaller towns often don't have the luxury of assigning community relations to a specific individual, but still receive calls from local groups and organizations asking for someone to speak to their group.

Now that you're an authority on con games — you *did* read this book, didn't you? — you will be able to put together an interesting, informative presentation that will meet your department's community relations objectives and, quite possibly, enhance your own standing in the community as well.

Identifying the audience

The first thing to consider in planning your presentation is to ask yourself the question, "Who is the audience?"

If you'll be talking to a group of senior citizens, you'll want to slant the talk to topics of interest to them. For example, most con games, discussions of faith-healers, Gypsy cons and home-repair frauds would be suitable topics for discussion.

If you're talking to a civic group, such as the Lions, Rotary or Kiwanis, for example, you might discuss certain con games, crooked carnival games or the techniques of shortchange artists or pickpockets.

If you're speaking to a teenage audience, your talk might emphasize satanic cults or how teenagers who work in various retail outlets are often the victims of shortchange artists.

The point here is to carefully consider your audience, then let that determine your choice of material.

Planning your presentation

Once you've identified your audience, you can begin planning your presentation.

"Wait a minute," you say. "I can't talk for an hour!"

An hour might seem like a long time if you're not accustomed to public speaking, but with questions and answers, you won't even have enough time to cover everything you might like to.

We recommend that you limit your presentation to two or three major topics.

Let's assume that you want to cover three topics: con games, faith-healers and fortune tellers, and techniques of pickpockets. If you plan to allow 15 minutes for each topic, and another 10 minutes for questions and answers, then five minutes for introductory and closing remarks, you'll have a well-balanced one-hour program.

If you break the time down this way, you'll quickly discover that you don't have a lot of time to cover any one area in detail. Actually, you really don't want to in this situation — you're providing an overview of the topic, not an in-depth analysis.

It's possible, of course, to limit your presentation to information on a single topic — con games, for example. In that case, you'll have the time to go into more detail on a specific con game, or provide more examples of other swindles. That decision is yours. But again, remember to consider the needs of your audience. What kind of information do they want, on what topic(s) and how much?

Questions from the audience

Your audience will be fascinated with what you have to tell them. The topic of con games is, in itself, an interesting one and your discussion can be expected to provoke many questions or, frequently, personal accounts of how that individual (or a friend, relative) was involved in a con game.

You have two options on how to handle questions and comments from the audience: (1) take the questions as they come during the presentation, or (2) ask the audience to hold all questions until the end of your presentation.

How you handle questions is a matter of personal preference. If you're more comfortable going through your complete presentation before taking questions, then by all means do so.

On the other hand, if you don't mind interruptions as you're discussing a certain topic, then ask for questions at any time. Bear in mind that answering questions in the middle of your presentation can have a tendency to get you "off track" if you're not careful.

Make sure that you're comfortable enough with your material so that you are able to answer the questions that arise. You should be able to give a direct, straightforward answer to just about any question that comes up. In addition to material covered in this book, other references in the bibliography will provide you with the background you need.

However, should someone describe a con game or a situation that's unknown to you, there's nothing wrong with saying, "That's a new one to me. Would you mind coming up to talk with me about that after the lecture?"

If you take the time to listen to personal accounts and descriptions of con games as recalled by audience members, you will learn a lot. Take time to listen to the audience members, and make notes later. You'll find your audience to be a great source of information.

Visual aids

Anytime you can use a visual aid to illustrate a point you're making, it's a plus. Almost any visual element will help reinforce the point you're trying to make.

For example, if you're discussing faith-healing, bring a willing volunteer up on stage and demonstrate how the short-leg routine works.

If you're talking about crooked carnival games, having a crooked game available for demonstration purposes will be viewed with considerable interest by your audience.

When you're discussing con games, show evidence of physical items used. For example, prepare an envelope or a bag as it might be used in the pigeon drop, with money or shredded newspaper inside. Hold up three walnut-shell halves when you're discussing the Three-Shell Game. Demonstrate how envelopes can be switched when you're discussing the Jamaican Switch.

Anything you can present that will visually reinforce what you're saying will greatly increase the interest of your audience.

Another technique is to outline key discussion points, then use an overhead projector to present them.

As you know, the lay public loves to hear police "war stories." Your presentation will be greatly enhanced if you can relate personal episodes relating to the topic at hand.

Local stories about arrests or convictions, con artists you have interrogated and similar episodes will peak the interest of your audience.

Basic Presentation Outline/Cue Sheet

The following outline/cue sheet is a suggested starting point for organizing your presentation. We suggest that you write out a similar list on a 5x7" index card before each engagement. It will help keep you on track and organized.

1. Welcome to audience, thank them for attending.
2. Introduce yourself by name, rank, experience, etc.
3. Explain what topic(s) you are going to deal with.
4. Tell the audience that you welcome questions (as you present the material, or held until the conclusion).
5. Presentation of topics, in order of importance.
6. Questions and/or closing comments.
7. Thank the audience for attending and for their attention.
8. Offer any handout material, if available.

This basic format will serve you well.

Suggested topics

Any chapter in this book can provide you with suitable material for a topic. Many fit into logical categories. Pickpockets and shortchange artists, for example, seem to work well together as topic material. Fortune tellers, psychics, channelers and fraudulent spiritualists all have common ties.

Home-repair scams and crimes against the elderly can easily be combined into a single topic.

One caution: the topic of satanic cults can be an awkward one. Many people may find this topic too controversial and/or objectionable. It might also be a difficult topic for you to cover if you have not had personal experience with investigating cult-related crimes. Our advice: if you're at all unsure, don't open it up as a topic.

Outlining

Once you have selected the topic(s) you're planning to present, the next step is to arrange the material into a logical sequence, using an outline. Here is an example of how you might structure an outline for a presentation of con games:

1. What is a con?
    a. Specialized kind of cheating
    b. Con artist always has a method for controlling the outcome
    c. Most con games are well-rehearsed plots
    d. Con games play on the victim's greed or good nature
    e. In some con games, the victim is convinced he or she is committing a crime
    f. There is always a method for the victim to freely give his or her money to the con artist
2. Why do people fall victim to con game schemes?
    a. The victim believes he or she may be getting something for nothing (greed), or
    b. The victim believes he or she is helping someone in authority (good nature)
    c. Large amounts of money or valuable merchandise are shown to the victim

       d. The con artist's ability to play the role convincingly
3. Two basic types of con games
       a. Short con — a quick, simple con played out in a matter of minutes or hours for whatever money or valuables the victim may have or can easily obtain
       b. Big con — an elaborate con stretching out days, weeks or even months, but only used when the final payoff would involve a substantial amount of money.

From this point, you discuss how particular con games work. Start with the most popular con games currently being worked in your city or town.

Take time to explain how the con game is set up, how and why it happens, and what the final result is. Your objective is to explain the con so that the average person in the audience can understand how it works. As mentioned earlier, it isn't necessary to go into great detail. If your explanation isn't clear or if someone wants more detail, they will ask for that during the question and answer period.

At the end of your presentation, recommend several books for those who would like additional information. You'll be surprised at how many people will jot down the titles.

You might also recommend movies, in which con games are a significant part of the plot. Most people have seen The Sting, which is an elaborate big con. Another good movie is House of Games, currently available in video stores for home viewing.

Using handout materials

Your audience will be most appreciative if you have handout material available. Check the Resources section of this book for suggested sources.

If you can't provide material from outside sources, consider typing up brief notes on the subject matter you discussed on your own, and duplicating them for distribution. One or two pages would be sufficient, and would reinforce your message. Attach your business card to the material.

Overcoming nervousness

If you are new to public speaking, keep a few things in mind. People want you to do well; they are on your side. Even before you start, you will have their respect and admiration, and you will be viewed as a subject matter expert who can help them understand a topic about which they have only vague knowledge.

Remember: you're in control of this situation, just as you are on your job.

Take your time. Talk slowly, loudly and clearly. If you're in a room without a microphone and an amplification system, project your voice as though you're speaking to the person in the last row of the audience.

That way you'll be sure that people are hearing you.

Make sure that you speak clearly. There is nothing worse than a speaker who cannot be understood. Perhaps you've been in an audience under those circumstances. Remember how quickly you lost interest in what the speaker had to say, simply because you couldn't understand what he or she was saying?

If you experience "stage fright," understand that it's a normal reaction for everyone, including seasoned professionals who spend their lives in front of an audience or a camera.

Here's a hint that you may find helpful. Just prior to going on, stand off by yourself. Close your eyes and relax. Take ten slow, deep breaths of air. This technique will really calm those butterflies in your stomach. As former television newsman Walter Cronkite noted, "You'll never get rid of the butterflies; the trick is getting them to fly in formation."

Public speaking can be a rewarding experience. Some people seem to have a knack for it, others have to work at it.

Regardless of which category you're in, when you're in front of the audience, if you talk enthusiastically about your subject matter and enjoy what you're doing, the effect will be contagious. Your audience will respond accordingly.

Resources

There are several groups and organizations available to help you if you have questions or need assistance in certain areas.

Committee for the Scientific Investigation of Claims of the Paranormal. CSICOP is an organization that, according to its statement of purpose, "attempts to encourage the critical investigation of paranormal and fringe-science claims from a responsible, scientific point of view and to disseminate factual information about the results of such inquiries to the scientific community and the public." There are numerous local, regional and national groups with aims similar to CSICOP and, although they work in cooperation with CSICOP, they are independent and autonomous. The official journal of CSICOP is *The Skeptical Inquirer*, published quarterly. At the time this book went to press, an annual subscription was $22.50. For further information, write to *The Skeptical Inquirer*, Box 229, Buffalo, NY 14215.

CompuServe Information Service. If you're a computer-literate cop, have a personal computer, a modem and subscribe to CompuServe, you can tap into the Paranormal Issues section of CompuServe's Issues Forum. The forum area provides a gathering place for debating and obtaining the latest news and discussing things like UFOs, ESP, channeling and Tarot card reading. Believers and skeptics are both welcome to participate. There are no set topics for discussion — whatever is current and controversial usually surfaces for discussion. Currently, conferences on topics of interest are scheduled for Sundays at 8 p.m. Eastern Standard Time. For further information, contact CompuServe Corporate Headquarters, 5000 Arlington Centre Blvd., Columbus, OH 43220. Or, if you're already a member, (GO ISSUES) will get you started.

Cult Crime Impact Network. CCIN is a private, non-profit corporation, headquartered in Boise, Idaho. The primary purpose of the group is to "collect information about cult/occult motivation crimes for presentation to the law enforcement community." CCIN publishes the *File 18 Newsletter*, a participative publication. Most of the reports and training information are contributed by the readership. The *File 18 Newsletter* mailing list includes more than 1,500 people — most of them police officers or professionals in related fields. CCIN and two other groups hosted a five-day Ritualistic Crime seminar in Boise during October 1988. For further information on CCIN, contact Lt. Larry Jones, CCIN, Inc., 222 N. Latah St., Boise, ID 83706.

The National Association of Bunco Investigators, Inc. NABI is a non-profit organization composed of law enforcement officers who investigate swindle and fraud offenses and others in related fields. The organization publishes a bi-weekly bulletin which is confidential and intended for law enforcement use only. At the time this book went to press, annual membership dues were $25. For a membership application blank or further information, contact The National Association of Bunco Investigators, Inc., 400 E. Pratt Street, Suite 800, Baltimore, MD 21202.

Professionals Against Confidence Crime. PACC is a non-profit organization of professional law enforcement personnel who share information on confidence games and the con artists who practice them. PACC bulletins are confidential, for police use only, and are published whenever enough information on confidence activity is available. Their second annual seminar, a three-day conference, was held in December 1988 in Schaumburg, Ill. For further information, contact Sgt. Larry Miller, Professionals Against Confidence Crime, 20500 South Cicero, Matteson, IL 60443.

At times, you will find yourself involved with a case that falls outside your jurisdiction. Or, during your investigation, you may find that no criminal offense has occurred or that you are unable to meet the elements of the crime. In those cases, you may be able to refer the victim to one or more of the following agencies for assistance. They may also be of assistance to you in investigating your case.

Council of Better Business Bureaus. The Better Business Bureaus (BBB) mediate disputes between consumers and businesses. Contact: Council of Better Business Bureaus, 1514 Wilson Blvd., Arlington, VA 22209 (to find your nearest local office). The BBB also is a good source for printed material on con games, consumer fraud and home-repair scams to hand out during lectures.

Federal Trade Commission. The FTC investigates investment fraud and consumer fraud. Contact: Bureau of Consumer Protection, Federal Trade Commission, Washington, D.C. 20580.

Food and Drug Administration. The FDA gets involved with claims of "miracle" health products and medical quackery. Contact: Consumer Affairs Office, Food and Drug Administration, 5600 Fishers Lane, Rockville, MD 20857.

Securities and Exchange Commission. The SEC investigates fraud involving securities (stocks, bonds and similar financial investments).

Contact: Securities and Exchange Commission, Office of Consumer Affairs and Information Services, 450 Fifth St. NW, Washington, D.C. 20549; or 202-272-7450.

United States Postal Service. The postal service inspectors are always interested in investigating cases where it appears that the mails have been used to defraud. Contact: The Postal Inspector in Charge, P.O. Box 96096, Washington, D.C. 20066-6096. There may also be an inspector in your area.

Locally, you may be able to refer the victim to one of these agencies for assistance:

The local chapter of the Better Business Bureau,

The local District Attorney's office,

The Office of the Attorney General in your state,

The local office of the American Medical Association,

Various consumer action groups in your city or state,

Newspaper "Action Line" columns or consumer help segments on local TV shows,

Your state's Department of Revenue (for fraud regarding state taxes, cigarette taxes and amusement device taxes and licensing, and lottery fraud),

Your state's Department of Public Aid (for cases of welfare fraud).

Glossary

Here are some of the more common terms used by various con artists and swindlers, crooked carnival store operators and other cheats.

Alibi agent — The operator of a crooked carnival game of skill who keeps the mark playing by providing alibis as to why the person hasn't won yet and offers advice for the next attempt.

Alibi store — A crooked carnival game of skill that cannot be won, although the operator leads the victim to believe he or she can win.

Beef — A complaint by the victim about being defrauded.

Belly joint — A crooked carnival game that is controlled by the operator who leans against the counter with his stomach.

Big con — An elaborately staged confidence game, often taking place over days or weeks, in order to obtain a significant amount of money from the victim(s). The big con involves a number of con artists in various roles. Opposite of "short con."

Bilk — Synonymous with cheating, swindling or defrauding a person.

Blowoff — Any technique used by a con artist to get rid of the mark at the successful conclusion of a con game.

Broad tosser — The person who controls the cards in the Three-Card Monte game.

Burn the lot — A crooked carnival that has defrauded the people of a particular town so badly that another carnival will be unable to come in later is said to have "burned the lot."

Carny workers — People who work in a carnival. Also known as "carnies."

Cold reading — A technique used by fortune tellers and others to "size up" a person by his or her responses and channel future statements in the direction the person has unknowingly indicated.

Count store — A crooked carnival game in which the player gets numbers that are added by the operator and converted into a total score.

Dip — Slang for pickpocket.

Earnest money — The "good faith" money requested from victims in certain con games.

Flat store — A crooked carnival game. The operator of a flat store is known as a "flattie."

Gaff — Any alteration to a carnival game or other gambling device that favors the operator in a game of chance.

Grifter — Another name for a professional cheat or con artist.

Grind joint — Any carnival game that keeps grinding away at a player's money until it is all gone.

Hot seat game — A card game where every player is a part of the swindle except the victim.

Hustler — A gambling cheat.

Mark — The person who has been set up as the victim or intended victim of a con game or crooked carnival game.

Nail joint — A crooked carnival game where the player attempts to drive a nail into a board with just one blow of a hammer.

Patch — The person in the management of the carnival who has the job of dealing with any problems between the carnival and the local authorities.

P.C. joint — A P.C. joint is a carnival game that has a mathematical percentage (P.C.) built in to favor it.

Peek store — A crooked carnival game in which the operator peeks at the selected number, covering one of the digits, if necessary, when showing it to the player.

Scam — Synonymous with con, swindle, fraud

(the) Send — The point in a con game where the victim is sent to get more money.

Short con — A con game played out in a matter of minutes, hours or days. Opposite of "big con."

Single-o — Any hustler or cheat who works without a partner.

(the) Sting — The point in any con game when the victim is relieved of his or her money.

Straight — A carnival game that is operated honestly is said to be "straight."

Tarot — A deck of 78 cards divided into two parts: the Major Arcana and the Minor Arcana. The cards are considered to be a method for divining the past, the present and the future. Those who use these cards are called "Tarot card readers."

Telling the tale — The con artist's explanation of the circumstances and how the mark will profit.

Town clowns — How carnival game operators refer to the local police.

Townies — How carnival game operators refer to the local townspeople.

Two-way store — Any carnival game that can be run either crooked or straight, depending on how the operator chooses.

With it — A term used by one carnival worker to another to let him know he's in the same business. "I'm with it," he will say.

Selected Reading

The authors have compiled this bibliography for those who wish to explore the subjects discussed in this book in greater detail. Many of these books can be found in local bookstores or public libraries. Others may be obtained directly from the publisher. Unfortunately, some of the older titles are out-of-print.

Adams, M. P. *The Rich Uncle from Fiji*. Melbourne, Australia: The Exchange Press, 1911. Reprinted by Gambler's Book Club of Las Vegas.

Blackstone, Jr., Harry. *There's One Born Every Minute*. Los Angeles: J. P. Tarcher, Inc., 1976.

Blum, Richard H. *Deceivers and Deceived*. Springfield, Ill.: Charles C Thomas, 1972.

Booth, John. *Psychic Paradoxes*. Los Alamitos, Calif.: Ridgeway Press, 1984.

Bowyer, J. Barton. *Cheating*. New York: St. Martin's Press, 1982.

Brandon, Ruth. *The Spiritualists*. Buffalo, N.Y.: Prometheus Books, 1984.

Brannon, W. T. *The Con Game and "Yellow Kid" Weil*. New York: Dover Publications, Inc., 1974.

Capaldi, Nicholas. *The Art of Deception*. Buffalo, N.Y.: Prometheus Books, 1987.

Dunninger, Joseph. *Inside the Medium's Cabinet*. New York: David Kemp and Company, Inc., 1935.

Dunninger, Joseph. *What's on Your Mind?* Cleveland: The World Publishing Company, 1944.

Edsall, F. S. *The World of Psychic Phenomena*. New York: Bell Publishing Company, 1958.

Fairley, John and Welfare, Simon. *Arthur C. Clarke's World of Strange Powers*. New York: G. P. Putnam's Sons, 1984.

Fisher, John. *Never Give A Sucker An Even Break*. New York: Pantheon Books, 1976.

Foster, William Trufant. *Gyps and Swindles*. New York: Public Affairs Committee, Inc., 1945.

Frazier, Kendrick (edited by). *Science Confronts the Paranormal*. Buffalo, N.Y.: Prometheus Books, 1986.

Freedland, Nat. *The Occult Explosion*. New York: G. P. Putnam's Sons, 1972.

Gibson, Walter. *The Bunco Book*. Holyoke, Mass.: Sidney H. Radner, 1946.

Gibson, Walter. *Carnival Gaffs*. Las Vegas: Gambler's Book Club, 1976.

Gibson, Walter (edited by). *The Fine Art of Swindling*. New York: Grosset & Dunlap, Inc., 1966.

Godwin, John. *This Baffling World*. New York: Hart Publishing Company, Inc., 1968.

Gordon, Henry. *ExtraSensory Deception*. Buffalo, N.Y.: Prometheus Books, 1987.

Gordon, Henry. *Channeling Into The New Age*. Buffalo, N.Y.: Prometheus Books, 1988.

Gresham, William Lindsay. *Monster Midway*. New York: Rinehart and Company, Inc., 1948.

Gresham, William Lindsay. *Nightmare Alley*. New York: Rinehart and Company, Inc., 1946.

Harris, Melvin. *Investigating the Unexplained*. Buffalo, N.Y.: Prometheus Books, 1986.

Henderson, M. Allen. *Flimflam Man: How Con Games Work*. Boulder, Colo.: Paladin Press, 1985.

Henderson, M. Allen. *Money for Nothing: Rip-Offs, Cons and Swindles*. Boulder, Colo.: Paladin Press, 1986.

Hoy, David. *The Meaning of Tarot*. Nashville: Aurora Publishers, Inc., 1971.

Houdini, Harry. *Miracle Mongers And Their Methods*. New York: E. P. Dutton and Company, 1920.

Houdini, Harry. *Houdini — A Magician Among The Spirits*. New York: Arno Press, 1972.

Houdini, Harry. *The Right Way To Do Wrong*. Boston: Harry Houdini, 1906.

Hull, Burling. *The Billion Dollar Bait*. Deland, Fla.: Volcanda Associates, 1977.

Jacques, Pierre. *Complete Course in Pick Pocketing*. New York: Tannen Magic, 1983.

James, H. K. *The Destruction of Mephisto's Greatest Web*. Salt Lake City: The Raleigh Publishing Co., 1914.

Joseph, Eddie. *How to Pick Pockets*. Colon, Mich.: Abbott's Magic Co., 1940.

Keene, M. Lamar. *The Psychic Mafia*. New York: St. Martin's Press, 1975.

Klass, Philip. *UFOs: The Public Deceived*. Buffalo, N.Y.: Prometheus Books, 1983.

Klass, Philip. *UFO-Abductions, A Dangerous Game*. Buffalo, N.Y.: Prometheus Books, 1988.

Kurtz, Paul (edited by). *A Skeptic's Handbook to Parapsychology*. Buffalo, N.Y.: Prometheus Books, 1985.

Lindberg, Gary. *The Confidence Man in American Literature*. New York: Oxford University Press, 1982.

MacDougall, Curtis D. *Hoaxes*. New York: Dover Publications, 1958.

Marshall, Frances (compiled by). *Wanna Bet?* Chicago: Magic. Inc., 1969.

Maurer, David W. *Language of the Underworld*. Lexington, Ky.: The University Press of Kentucky, 1981.

Maurer, David W. *The American Confidence Man*. Springfield, Ill.: Charles C Thomas, 1974.

Mayer, Ralph. *Short Changing*. Colon, Mich.: Abbott's Magic, n.d.

Miall, Agnes M. *The Book of Fortune Telling*. New York: Crescent Books, 1987.

Nickell, Joe. *Secrets of the Supernatural*. Buffalo, N.Y.: Prometheus Books, 1988.

Ortiz, Darwin. *Gambling Scams*. New York: Dodd, Mead & Company, 1984.

Partridge, Eric. *A Dictionary Of The Underworld*. New York: The Macmillan Company, 1950.

Rachum, Joseph. *Short Changing*. 1941.

Randi, James. *Flim-Flam!* Buffalo, N.Y.: Prometheus Books, 1982.

Randi, James. *The Faith Healers*. Buffalo, N.Y.: Prometheus Books, 1987.

Rogers, Mike. *The Complete Mike Rogers*. Chicago: Magic, Inc., 1975.

Scarne, John. *Scarne's Complete Guide to Gambling*. New York: Simon and Schuster, 1961.

Sheaffer, Robert. *The UFO Verdict*. Buffalo, N.Y.: Prometheus Books, 1980.

Sorrows, Gene. *All About Carnivals*. North Miami, Fla.: American Federation of Police, 1985.

Stowers, Carlton. *The Unsinkable Titanic Thompson*. Burnet, Texas: Eakin Press, 1982.

Van Rensselaer, Alexander. *Betcha Can't Do It!* New York: D. Appleton-Century Company, Inc., 1940.

Villiod, Eugene. *Crooks, Con Men and Cheats*. Las Vegas: Gambler's Book Club, 1980.

Wooldridge, Clifton R. *The Devil and the Grafter.* Chicago: Clifton R. Wooldridge, 1907.

Afterthoughts

The authors hope the information in this book will help you to identify, arrest and bring to trial the con artists, swindlers and other "bad guys" who perpetrate these frauds on the average citizen.

Your understanding of how these con games go down can enhance your credibility as an expert witness when such cases go to trial.

In *STING SHIFT*, we have attempted to identify most of the common and frequently worked con games that you might encounter in your work. The authors would be interested in learning of your successes.

We would be particularly interested in knowing of any other new or unusual scams you encounter, or current twists on old frauds. Please write directly to the authors in care of:

Street-Smart Communications
7275 South Depew Street
Littleton, CO 80123

About the authors

Lindsay Smith has 23 years of writing and editing experience in the public relations departments of three major corporations. Currently, he is a writer and editor for U S WEST Communications, a subsidiary of U S WEST, Inc.

Smith has had a life-long interest in magic, and is a member of the International Brotherhood of Magicians, the Society of American Magicians and the Magic Collectors' Association.

He was graduated from Marshall University, Huntington, W.Va., with a B.A. degree in journalism. He lives in Littleton, Colo., with his wife, Donna, and their four teenage children: Brad, Debi, Jennifer and Kimberly.

Bruce Walstad is a 13-year veteran of the police department in Franklin Park, Ill. For the past four years, he has been a detective in that department.

Walstad is a member of the American Society of Law Enforcement Trainers, and is a member of the Legal Committee of The Committee for the Scientific Investigation of Claims of the Paranormal. He also is a member of the International Brotherhood of Magicians and the Society of American Magicians, and has been performing magic professionally since 1969. Walstad presents a seminar, "Cons, Scams and Crooked Carnival Games," for law enforcement professionals nationwide.

He lives in Franklin Park, Ill., with his wife, Pat, and their six-year-old son John.

What others say about *STING SHIFT:*

"*STING SHIFT is a valuable guide to law enforcement officers investigating cons. After studying this book, officers will be armed with the knowledge to interview victims and suspects intelligently. With this book, and a little practical experience, law enforcement may be able to shift the 'sting' from the victim to the con artist.*"

— Special Agent Arthur Eberhart,
The FBI Law Enforcement Bulletin, May 1989
Washington, D.C.

"*This concisely written book is a virtual encyclopedia of con games. Were this book devoid of practical value, I would still enthusiastically recommend it for its interest and entertainment value. But it is much more. It is an informative expose that affects your financial and emotional well-being.*

I highly recommend STING SHIFT *for your reading enjoyment, for your information and for your life-saving protection.*"

— Bob Steiner,
Fellow, The Committee for the Scientific Investigation of Claims of the Paranormal,
Past national president, Society of American Magicians
and author, *Don't Get Taken!*

"*Fascinating, must-reading, since con men use the techniques to steal millions from the unsuspecting.*"

— Howard Schwartz,
Director of Marketing,
Gambler's Book Club, Las Vegas

"*STING SHIFT is excellent. Very complete and thorough. The book should have a wide appeal among many magicians.*"

— Sid Lorraine,
writer, columnist
Toronto, Canada

"Your book provides valuable insight into common scams law enforcement officers must be aware of. It will be an important addition to North East Multi-Regional Training's Resource Center."

— Frank Johnson,
Field Operations Coordinator,
North East Multi-Regional Training

"Several of the chapters cover topics of interest to magicians — con games, shortchanging, crooked carnival games, pickpocketing methods, etc. — and I highly recommend this well-illustrated book. Fascinating and informative reading."

— Walt Hudson, columnist
The New Tops, March 1989

"STING SHIFT is great! I read it from cover to cover and was amazed to discover the various scams and cons that go on everywhere in our country (and the world). I am proud to have my drawings included in the book."

— Ed Harris,
artist, cartoonist
Minneapolis

"STING SHIFT is written for the street cop, in the street cop's language, by a street cop. The information contained in this book will assist the officers in identification, investigation and indictment of the 'con' man."

— Detective Tom Beaver,
Office of the District Attorney
Denver

"This book is a warehouse of valuable information, and any police trainer who desires to increase his knowledge of cons, swindles and pseudoscience will want a copy. It is well worth the price."

— *The ASLET Journal,*
American Society of Law Enforcement Trainers
March/April 1989